A New View
of Retirement

James F. Locke

A New View *of* Retirement

Transforming

Investment

Strategies

from **Growth**

to Income

Advantage | Books

Published by Advantage Books, Charleston, South Carolina.
An imprint of Advantage Media.

ADVANTAGE is a registered trademark, and the Advantage colophon is a trademark of Advantage Media Group, Inc.

Printed in the United States of America.

10 9 8 7 6 5 4 3 2 1

ISBN: 979-8-89188-160-0 (Hardcover)

Library of Congress Control Number: 2025906557

Cover design by Matthew Morse.
Layout design by Megan Elger.

This publication is designed to provide accurate and authoritative information in regard to the subject matter covered. It is sold with the understanding that the publisher is not engaged in rendering legal, accounting, or other professional services. If legal advice or other expert assistance is required, the services of a competent professional person should be sought.

Advantage Books is an imprint of Advantage Media Group. Advantage Media helps busy entrepreneurs, CEOs, and leaders write and publish a book to grow their business and become the authority in their field. Advantage authors comprise an exclusive community of industry professionals, idea-makers, and thought leaders. For more information go to **advantagemedia.com**.

Investment advisory services offered through Sound Income Strategies, LLC, an SEC registered investment advisor firm. Poole Locke Associates and Sound Income Strategies, LLC are not associated entities. Poole Locke Associates is a franchisee of the Retirement Income Source. The Retirement Income Source and Sound Income Strategies, LLC are associated entities.

CONTENTS

INTRODUCTION

S ome people know exactly what they want to do with their lives, even if it's just a dream—perhaps it's to be an astronaut, a fireman, or president of the United States. Growing up, I wanted to be a center fielder for the New York Yankees. Since the center fielder position was taken, I decided to focus on other things. I can't sit here and tell you that I had every intention of helping people focus on their transition to retirement, from accumulating assets to learning how to distribute those assets over thirty years or more, but here I am.

I liked math and science, and, even at a young age, I was really good at listening patiently, getting my point across in conversation, and helping people. I was also a camp counselor in high school. While my mom, who taught second grade, thought those traits and experiences would make me a good teacher as well, I knew that I would never make my fortune in that field. Instead, I entered the mechanical engineering program at Villanova University, following more in my dad's footsteps. He was a chemical engineer and one of the smartest people I have ever known. However, I struggled through that program for two years before switching to business administration with a focus on finance and financial markets.

After graduating from college, I wasn't too particular about what job I wanted to take, so I ended up working at an insurance company with a tyrannical leader and a terrible culture. On my first day on the job, I saw the woman who had hired me exit the boss's office in tears and then leave for the day, only to return the next day as if nothing had happened. It was utter chaos, and I knew I wasn't going to last long there.

Three weeks later, a man named Roger called me. He had received one of the dozens of résumés I had sent when answering job ads in *The New York Times* (this was before internet job searching). The job was to be a stock options trader. I didn't know if I had a real chance but was excited to be going to the New York Stock Exchange for an interview. During the interview, Roger asked me a few questions about my background and explained that the job started as a clerk with training in options trading, and, if I did well, then I would ultimately become an actual options trader.

When Roger pulled a second person into the interview, it turned into a series of odd, rapid-fire questions, such as, "What is the distance from Earth to the moon?" No way was I going to answer, "I have no idea," so I started doing the math in my head. I figured light travels at around two hundred thousand miles per second, and it takes about eight seconds for light to travel from the moon to Earth. Taking that total, 1.6 million, and adjusting for numbers I had rounded, I answered, "The distance is 1.4 million miles." My answer was way off—it takes about 1.3 seconds for light to travel from Earth to the moon, a distance of 238,855 miles. It turned out that they didn't really care whether I knew the answer; they were only interested in whether I could use logic to come up with an answer and whether I could divide in sixteenths and then translate that into decimals. Those were the skills needed on the stock exchange.

I passed the first interview and then was taken to the balcony above the trading floor, where Roger left me with Charlie, the company owner. Charlie very briefly talked about the job and then asked one question: "Yankees or Mets?" For an instant, my dreams of being a center fielder came back, and I wondered if there would be less pressure on the baseball field than in this interview. Knowing the intense rivalry between the two teams and their fans, I had a sinking feeling that the answer to my question would make all the difference in landing the job.

Fortunately, before I could speak, a man next to Charlie laughingly commented about how much of a pain Charlie was. They were just having fun at my expense, and Charlie was using this as an opportunity to see how I behaved under pressure (It was working!). The man then told me to ignore Charlie and his antics, shook my hand, and walked away, saying, "The fact that you're even talking to him means you're about to get the job. Congratulations." Charlie confirmed that they would be happy to have me as their newest options trading clerk on the floor in Philadelphia.

In that role, I learned a lot about the markets and how they work. It was the first of several different positions with different firms until I became an independent options trader. Options traders often move between firms as opportunities to trade different equities become available. Moving firms has less to do with the company and its benefits and more to do with the earnings potential of being the lead market maker in a particular set of equity options.

In 2005, my financial backer decided he would rather race cars than work as an options trader, leaving me to look for yet another job. I found another financial backer to support me as an independent trader, but the options industry was changing with the introduction of multiple listings of options, rather than each exchange having its own equity option books. Plus, the introduction of black box trading systems by the big boys such as Goldman Sachs and Morgan Stanley meant that they had much more inside information than little individual market makers like me, which was something I wasn't particularly interested in combatting. My time of trading equity index options and proprietary index options came to an end. After that, I became a minority partner in a firm helping institutional investment managers organize data and write requests for proposals. That time in my life helped me learn more about the institutional investment side of the financial world. After many years, this company closed as well, and I found myself without full-time employment once again because of the decisions of others.

That was enough for me. I had reached a point in my career where I didn't want to work for someone else—for them to have such a say in my future. I didn't really enjoy institutional investing any longer, and I began to realize I could take what I had learned so far and help people avoid what had happened to my grandmother.

When her husband (my grandfather) died unexpectedly, she was forced to move back in with her mother. Without a pension, insurance, or other similar protections, my grandmother had no other choice than to go home to a one-bedroom, one-sink apartment in the shadow of the Empire State Building and raise her child (my mother) in that small space. Mae, my grandmother, had to go into the workforce that offered few protections for single/widowed mothers in the early 1940s. She had to work hard just to make ends meet. And she was one of the lucky ones because her mother was available to help her land on her feet and raise my mother.

Ultimately, my grandmother was able to stop working and live with my mother and our family. Growing up, I loved the fact that Grandma lived upstairs. She played with us and baked cookies for us. When I was older, I realized that her financial situation had been precarious her entire life. And because of her situation, my grand-

mother always urged my mother to take advantage of every opportunity available—education, pension, retirement accounts, employer
matching in 401(k) accounts, being part of a union—to ensure she
had a more secure future. This encouragement proved to be the best
advice she could have passed on. My mother took advantage of retirement planning because of my grandmother's encouragement and from
seeing how much Grandma struggled daily. Perhaps my grandmother's
financial retirement situation was not the best planned, but she sure
knew how to ensure my mother would not have the same financial
worries she had growing up. This ultimately helped my grandmother,
my mother, and even me.

So, with my grandmother in mind, I decided to switch to a career
in retirement planning. A friend of mine suggested that I talk to Jerry
Poole, a financial advisor whom he and his father had worked with.
I met Jerry at the restaurant where he had breakfast while reading
The New York Times five days a week. I wanted to learn about how to
break into the industry, so I was glad to have someone to talk to, but
as I got up to leave, Jerry asked me to have breakfast with him again
the next day. That's when he told me he was looking for someone he
could trust to be there for his clients after he was no longer able to
work full time. He was trying to find a way to transition his clients
into a good situation.

I went home and thought about it, and I ultimately decided that
God had placed Jerry in my life for a reason. We set up a partnership, Poole Locke Associates, LLC, and I began studying for the exams
to obtain the necessary licenses from the United States Securities and
Exchange Commission (SEC)—I passed all of them on my first attempt.

Today, I am SEC Series 65 licensed, and I manage all discretion-
ary accounts for my clients through Sound Income Strategies, LLC,
an SEC-registered investment advisor firm with more than $3 billion

in assets under management. I work with an enormous team at Sound Income Strategies who are true professionals in researching the best income-producing investments on the market.

My role at Sound Income Strategies is to help people who are near or in retirement to understand what their investments are, how much income their investments are producing, how much risk they're taking versus the risk they want to take, and that there's a right way and a wrong way to generate income in retirement. In short, I teach people.

I wrote this book to reach people who are about ten years from retirement or who are just beginning retirement. They have $100,000 to $5 million to invest and are concerned about things such as Social Security, taxes, required minimum distributions (RMDs), and more, and they are looking to improve their retirement situation. With the information in this book, I want to teach people how to transition from accumulating assets throughout their lives to a situation where they can set those assets up to distribute income for the rest of their lives. In retirement, the strategies that worked so well helping you accumulate assets could potentially backfire badly when used to distribute assets. Knowing how to transition will give you the peace of mind of knowing your assets will last longer than you! How do I help people make this transition? It all starts with the Retirement Risk Report (RRR) process. I will reference my RRR process many times throughout this book. Walking through the details of an RRR helps educate people about where the pitfalls in an existing plan might manifest and begins the conversation about how transitioning to investing for your phase in life allows for change.

So, in the end, as it turns out, my mother was correct. I am a teacher. Maybe not the same kind of teacher she thought I would be—rather than teaching basic math to six-, seven-, and eight-year-olds, I am teaching sixty-, seventy-, and eighty-year-olds about how to invest for income. That's something they don't teach in school. Thanks, Mom, for always pushing me to a place where I can flourish, a place where I help people realize that it's not about how much money you die with, but how you're living your life.

CHAPTER 1

TR = I + G—the Answer to Every Problem

Recently, I started working with a new client whose entire retirement portfolio was in cash because the last time he committed to investing, he placed all his money in the stock market. That was September 10, 2001. The next day, after the attacks on the World Trade Center, the stock market closed for the rest of the week, wrecking his plans. After that, he vowed that he would build his retirement fund solely on the amount of cash he could save, ignoring the long-term growth that smart investing could have helped him achieve. If he had worked with a financial advisor all that time instead, he would be far better off with a plan based on growth. Even if his plan had included growth, however, now that he is just a few years from retirement, he needs something different.

If you are like my client and racing toward retirement but don't want to trust your luck, then you can eliminate the luck factor by understanding this one equation: TR = I + G.

Total Return = Income (dividends/interest) + Growth

If you remember only one thing after reading this book, let it be this equation: TR = I + G. But why is it so important?

Well, during your accumulation years (you will often hear this called the accumulation phase), those years when you were working and making an income and building your retirement portfolio, you just wanted to make money on your money. All that time, you just wanted to get more total return (TR), and it didn't matter whether it came from G (growth) or I (income). But when you're nearing retirement (this will be referenced as the distribution phase), that focus must change. You need to transition from accumulating wealth to understanding how the wealth you've accumulated can bring you an income. That's where TR = I + G comes in. It's the answer to having a renewable resource, no matter the market conditions. It is the answer to a stress-free retirement.

As you approach retirement, how you invest is all-important. Most people think that if they put their money in the stock market and the market goes up, then those returns mean they will have more money to spend. But it doesn't have to be that way in order to have income when you reach retirement. You can also put money into the market and it can go down, but you can still spend the same amount of money—as long as you understand that what you are spending is the income. If you are investing for income, then it doesn't matter what happens in the stock market.

Today, the average person can expect to enjoy twenty or thirty years of retirement. If you take income from your principal during that time, then you'll find yourself with less and less money in your portfolio generating income—the interest you need for income. In other words, if you continue to invest solely for total return, your plan may backfire. But if your portfolio is structured to generate income from interest and dividends, then your principal can stay intact until you need it later, for inflation, healthcare, leaving a legacy to others—or just for the peace of mind of knowing that you aren't going to run out of money.

Investing for Income—the Sure Bet

The total return on your investment comes from two different pieces: income in the form of interest and dividends and return from growth, otherwise known as appreciation. Return from growth is what everyone gets excited about. When people think about investing, they look for investments that they think will skyrocket overnight; they buy a stock today for $100, thinking that tomorrow it will be worth $1,000. While income from interest and dividends is less exciting, it's far more predictable. Who cares about minuscule dividends or a small interest payment, you say? Well, my team and I at Sound Income Strategies do. If you want a stress-free retirement, you will care too.

It's like betting at the racetrack: When the long shot wins, everyone screams with excitement. Everyone thinks that the winner was smart about their bet. But they weren't smarter; they were just lucky—and just for that one race; they're not showing you the tickets for all the races they lost. So while G stands for growth, G can also stand for gambling, because investing for growth can be a win-or-lose strategy. But you know what isn't a lose strategy? Investing for income—that's the more secure bet. Sure, we all want our assets to grow. In fact, we actually need them to grow to keep up with things such as inflation and the cost of living. But at the end of the day, the only thing that matters in retirement is how much we get paid and how much income we get from our investments.

For most of our working lives, we don't really care where the return on our investments comes from. But once we are about ten years away from retirement, where the return comes from is critical. It can mean the difference between a retirement of ease or a retirement of worry, or perhaps no retirement at all—at least not the way you had envisioned. Yet, in my experience, most financial advisors and money managers continue to attempt to match or do better than the returns of the broad stock market, even once someone is nearing retirement. That's because their livelihood depends on it. And it's hard to blame them because they have families and responsibilities too. If a portfolio manager's mutual fund can't keep up with the S&P 500, investors will sell their shares and move on to something else. For that reason, a lot of money managers and advisors continually push their clients and investors up the risk curve, not because the client wants it but because the money manager has to in order to keep their job.

That is why Sound Income Strategies, the investment team that I am part of, is different. We're not focused on total return; we're focused on making the retirement of your dreams come true, and that only happens through generating predictable income to allow you to live out those dreams.

Will the Money Last as Long as You Do?

Often, at my educational webinars and workshops, I tell a story about a client of mine who didn't become a client until it was almost too late. Elaine was sixty years old when her husband died unexpectedly in 1999. They had all sorts of plans and dreams of what their retirement together would look like, but in an instant, those dreams were shattered. Although Elaine was devastated, the love of her children and grandchildren helped her through that difficult time, and she was encouraged, rightly so, to go ahead and retire—to just stick to her plan and live her retirement dream.

At that point, she went to her financial advisor, who worked for a large international company. She talked with him about the money that she would need to live the new retirement that she envisioned. She had a small pension and would eventually start collecting Social Security. In addition to those income sources, she was going to need another $40,000 per year. She had $1 million in an individual retirement account (IRA), and her advisor told her, "That's great. We will use the 4 percent rule in investing, which states that you can safely withdraw 4 percent of your assets from your portfolio and expect them to grow back each year." The investment advice that was used to grow her portfolio to $1 million worked so well that Elaine believed it would continue to work in her retirement. After all, her advisor was a professional, wasn't he? But using the same strategy for her in retirement was a mistake.

The strategies that work well for enabling you to accumulate money prior to retirement will backfire in a big way if you use them to distribute money to you during retirement. But off Elaine went, taking $40,000 a year out of her IRA. She was invested in "safe" exchange-traded funds and mutual funds that tracked the broad market indexes, such as the S&P 500 and the Dow Jones. Her advisor was not concerned because she was only going to be taking 4 percent out of her portfolio, and he knew that the stock market averages 9 percent over the long run. In fact, Elaine was told that she would have more money in ten years, so she did not worry about it.

In the table below, you can see what happened to Elaine's money over the first thirteen years of her retirement.

THE WITHDRAWAL METHOD

DATE	BEGINNING CASH	S&P 500 TOTAL RETURN	WITHDRAWAL	END CASH
1/2000	$1,000,000	−9.10%	$40,000	$871,496
1/2001	$871,496	−11.89%	$40,000	$728,734
1/2002	$728,734	−22.10%	$40,000	$531,372
1/2003	$531,372	28.68%	$40,000	$637,080
1/2004	$637,080	10.88%	$40,000	$663,272
1/2005	$663,272	4.91%	$40,000	$654,123
1/2006	$654,123	15.79%	$40,000	$713,949
1/2007	$713,949	5.49%	$40,000	$713,041
1/2008	$713,041	−37.00%	$40,000	$418,385
1/2009	$418,385	26.46%	$40,000	$480,779
1/2010	$480,779	15.06%	$40,000	$508,140
1/2011	$508,140	2.11%	$40,000	$479,099
1/2012	$479,099	16.00%	$40,000	$514,132

Returns calculated using month-end price of the S&P 500 Total Return index published by the Chicago Board Options Exchange (https://www.cboe.com/ tradable_products/sp_500/).

In 2013, Elaine came into our office. She was crying and asked for my partner, Jerry Poole, who was also her pastor. When Jerry asked her what was wrong, she said she had just gone to the doctor and was informed that she was in perfect health. "He told me I was just as healthy as I was when I was sixty, and that I could expect to live another thirty years!" Do you see why she was so upset? She had another thirty years to live but less than half the money she needed to get through it. If Elaine had a long-term care need, she would not have the extra money to spend on it. If we were to experience unexpected inflation, like we saw in the early 1980s and during the COVID-19 pandemic of the early 2020s, she would not have the extra money to spend. If she wanted to give some money to her children or grand-children during her lifetime, or leave some after she was gone, she wouldn't be able to do that either.

To figure out what happened to Elaine, we dug into her invest-ment accounts and found that she was invested for growth—but there had been no growth for thirteen years. In fact, as the graph below shows, the stock market was underwater for most of that time.

DOW JONES INDUSTRIAL AVERAGE— BULLS AND BEARS, 2000–2013

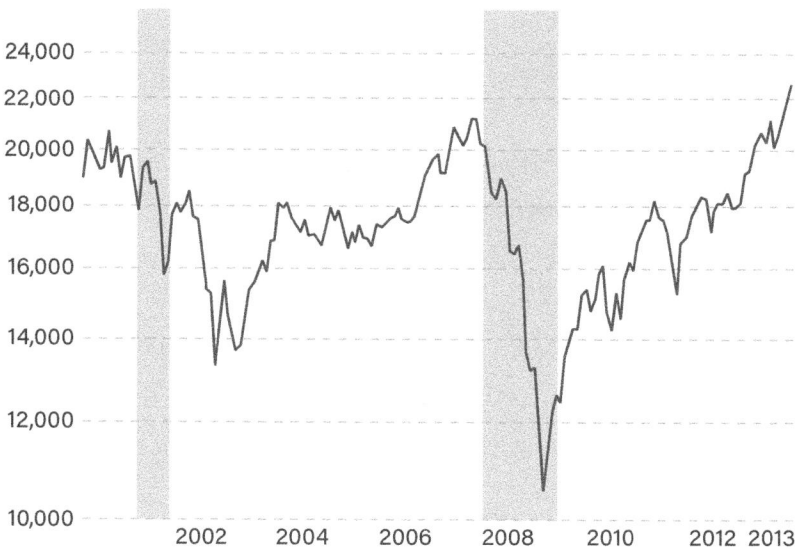

Source: "Dow Jones - DJIA - 100 Year Historical Chart," Historical Chart, Macrotrends, accessed June 2024, https://www.macrotrends.net/1319/ dow-jones-100-year-historical-chart.

In retirement, Elaine was using the same strategies to distribute her assets that had been used to accumulate them. She was relying on stock market growth, and when that wasn't there, she sold off shares of her investments to have the $40,000 she needed each year. Once you start selling off shares of your investments, you can end up selling off more and more as the stock market declines—this cannibalizes your principal.

For example, if a mutual fund costs $10 per share and you need $1,000 in one month from that mutual fund, you will have to sell one hundred shares of it. If that mutual fund drops in value from $10 to $5 per share, and you still need the $1,000 to live on, now you have to sell two hundred shares of your investment. When the mutual fund goes back up to $10 per share, guess what? You don't have as much money as you started with because you sold your shares. And what's worse is that you sold them when they were low, which is called reverse dollar cost averaging.

Fortunately, we were able to help Elaine restructure her portfolio so that it wasn't composed of investments that relied solely on growth but instead included investments that would provide predictable and reliable income. Unfortunately, for the second time in her life, her retirement dreams were shattered. No longer could she comfortably take $40,000 out of her portfolio every year because she was afraid that she would run out of money before she ran out of life.

The Difference TR = I + G Makes

Let's take a quick look at what options were available to Elaine back in 1999. If someone had explained TR = I + G to her, her situation would have looked very different thirteen years later.

The S&P 500 pays an annual dividend of 1.5 percent; this has been the payout for many decades. If she had taken out only the dividends on her investments—only what her portfolio actually earned—rather than crossing her fingers and toes and hoping that the stock market would grow appropriately and help her maintain her assets, she would still have had her principal in 2013. In the table below, you can see how, with some rounding, after thirteen years, her money would have been almost intact.

THE INCOME METHOD: SPENDING THE DIVIDEND ONLY ($15,000/YEAR)

DATE	BEGINNING CASH	S&P 500 TOTAL RETURN	**1.5% DIVIDEND	END CASH
1/2000	$1,000,000	−9.10%	$15,000	$894,909
1/2001	$894,909	−11.89%	$15,000	$773,850
1/2002	$773,850	−22.10%	$15,000	$589,209
1/2003	$589,209	28.68%	$15,000	$740,704
1/2004	$740,704	10.88%	$15,000	$805,132
1/2005	$805,132	4.91%	$15,000	$829,031
1/2006	$829,031	15.79%	$15,000	$943,663
1/2007	$943,663	5.49%	$15,000	$980,458
1/2008	$980,458	−37.00%	$15,000	$606,142
1/2009	$606,142	26.46%	$15,000	$748,431
1/2010	$748,431	15.06%	$15,000	$844,273
1/2011	$844,273	2.11%	$15,000	$847,187
1/2012	$847,187	16.00%	$15,000	$967,152

The 1.5 percent dividend return listed is not the actual S&P 500 dividend yield.
**This number is based on a hypothetical return of 1.5 percent.

Of course, the big problem here is that Elaine needed $40,000 per year to retire and she would only be getting $15,000 per year. She would be living on $25,000 less than she needed each year.

So what should have happened in 1999? Elaine's financial advisor should have known that investing is not a one-size-fits-all T-shirt. He should have understood that investing during the accumulation phase is different from investing for the distribution phase.

If Elaine had shifted how she invested and been able to generate a 4 percent dividend or more, then not only would she have had the income she needed during those thirteen years that the stock market was underwater but she would still have had all of her investment shares. The value of her portfolio would have fluctuated, but she would never have lost her principal because she would never have been forced to sell shares to meet her retirement income needs.

You can see in the chart below that, with an income specialist overseeing the portfolio instead of a growth-focused advisor, there is a better chance of achieving a stress-free retirement.

THE INCOME METHOD: SPENDING THE DIVIDEND ONLY ($40,000/YEAR)

DATE	BEGINNING CASH	S&P 500 TOTAL RETURN	**HYPO-THETICAL 4% DIVIDEND	END CASH
1/2000	$1,000,000	−9.10%	$40,000	$894,909
1/2001	$894,909	−11.89%	$40,000	$773,850
1/2002	$773,850	−22.10%	$40,000	$589,209
1/2003	$589,209	28.68%	$40,000	$740,704
1/2004	$740,704	10.88%	$40,000	$805,132
1/2005	$805,132	4.91%	$40,000	$829,031
1/2006	$829,031	15.79%	$40,000	$943,663
1/2007	$943,663	5.49%	$40,000	$980,458
1/2008	$980,458	−37.00%	$40,000	$606,142
1/2009	$606,142	26.46%	$40,000	$748,431
1/2010	$748,431	15.06%	$40,000	$844,273
1/2011	$844,273	2.11%	$40,000	$847,187
1/2012	$847,187	16.00%	$40,000	$967,152

The 4 percent dividend yield listed is not the actual S&P 500 dividend yield.
**This number is based on a hypothetical dividend of 4 percent.

Now, if Elaine has a long-term care need, if there is unforeseen inflation, or if she wants to give her money away or leave it as a legacy, she will have the principal available to use.

Portfolio Value Versus Income

A common belief I've found with my clients is that when the value of a portfolio drops, the income it produces also lowers. Of course, nothing is black and white, but the big picture shows that this is just not true; the value of your portfolio is not directly related to the income it produces. Let me give you an example.

In Delaware, where I'm located, people often buy beach houses as investments. They buy a beach house for $1 million, then they find a credit-worthy tenant who signs a contract to pay $50,000 in rent for the first year. That first year, if the value of real estate at the Delaware beaches has dropped by 10 percent, the value of the investment property will be $900,000. Yet, at the end of the year, the house has still generated $50,000 in rent.

Let's look at this real estate investment in terms of our equation: TR = I + G. The total return is –$50,000, made up of income of +$50,000 and growth of –$100,000. By all accounts, at the end of the first year, you should have less money than you started out with. But the $100,000 loss is only on paper. The house had a theoretical value of $1 million, and then it had a theoretical value of $900,000. Even though the portfolio (the house) is worth less money, you still have $50,000 in hand to spend. And you can spend it comfortably because you have a contract from your credit-worthy tenant who paid you cash to stay in the house. What's more, the tenant is going to pay you $50,000 in rent the next year too. So, in year two of owning the home, if its value increases by $100,000 and comes back to its original price of $1 million, guess how much rent you are going to collect? The same: $50,000.

Let's look at that equation again for the second year. Following TR = I + G, the total return is $150,000. The income is $50,000 and the growth is $100,000. The second year looks even better. Over the course of two years, you've been able to spend the same amount of money each year, even though, one year, your investment went down in value, and the next year, it went up in value. Either way, it didn't affect what you could spend, and the fact that you had a contract with a credit-worthy tenant gave you the comfort level to actually spend the money however you wanted. In this example, the ideal situation is that the value of the home goes up over the course of twenty or thirty years, but even if it does, guess what? You can never spend a dime of that money until you sell the house. The only thing you can spend along the way is the rental income.

If you're still unsure of the equation, think of it in terms of a chicken and eggs. When you have a chicken that lays eggs, you can eat the eggs every single day. But once you eat the chicken, there are no more eggs. Now imagine the chicken in this scenario is the principal in your portfolio and the eggs are your income from interest and dividends. Get the picture? (I wish I could take credit for this analogy, but it came from an industry mentor, Greg Melia in Oklahoma. Thanks, Greg!)

Another mentor of mine in this industry, Patrick Peason, someone whom I also look on as a friend, has a little jingle, and it makes me laugh every time because of its simplicity. He often sings it to his clients: "If you want your retirement to be stress-free, take from the *I* and not from the *G*."

I'll say it one last time: The solution to a stress-free retirement comes down to the simple equation TR = I + G. It's really that simple. In fact, my hope is that, if you decide to put this book down after reading this chapter and you never read another word of it, you can confidently walk away knowing how your money should be invested so that you can live a stress-free retirement. All you need is enough interest and dividends, and your money will last longer than you, letting you live the retirement of your dreams.

Ask Yourself ...

1. Where is my return coming from: how much from the I and how much from the G?

2. Is my financial advisor trained in investing for growth or investing for income?

3. Am I eating only my eggs or am I killing some of my chickens?

CHAPTER 2

Living the Dream

A s an income specialist, I have the responsibility of working with my clients to help ensure they can meet their expenses today and in the future. Part of my responsibility is to think of things that might happen to derail their retirement, things that haven't occurred to them. A good place to start is with an RRR. We use this at Sound Income Strategies to look at what you need and want from your income, where your money is allocated, the taxable status of your accounts, where your risk is, and more. My goal is to help you figure out how not to lose this "game of life," as one of my colleagues calls it. Let me explain.

When we talk to people about retirement and how to invest, we sometimes find that they actually have all they really need to enjoy retirement. For one couple, with around $2 million, we looked at what they wanted out of retirement, how much it was going to cost, and whether their plans would pay for their dreams. Looking at the whole picture, they had already "won." They had made it to retirement and had a plan that would fund their dreams. Why would they want to continue to invest aggressively in an attempt to double or triple what they had? There was no need to risk gambling with it. They'd already won.

Dream of Your Retirement

Generally speaking, most people could probably live on less income in retirement if they had to, but when they really begin to dream about their retirement, the idea of living on half of their income is never the primary goal, certainly not for any of my clients. How to dream for retirement is a very important part of the retirement process. Rather than focusing on the worst-case scenario people often think about—*What happens if I lose all my money? Will I be able to survive?*—my goal is to help people live their dreams.

Gone are the days of lifetime pensions when you knew how much steady income you were going to have. We now live in a world where we must save all we can and create our own pensions. Watching our portfolios swing from market highs to market lows can be nerve-racking. How much can you take out of your savings to live the retirement of your dreams?

Well, how big can you dream? That's where I spend half my time with new clients. I teach them (thanks, Mom) how to dream for those days beyond their working years. For example, when a new client comes in—let's say it's a couple—they may have all kinds of plans to travel and rent beach houses and invite their family because they have the peace of mind of knowing they have a renewable resource coming in. Let's say they have $5,000 per month from a pension and they are also getting $5,000 per month from Social Security, giving them a total of $10,000 per month. They very clearly have two sources of income that they can rely on, and both are pools of money that continue to earn more money and pay it out. Now, compare this to another couple who have no guaranteed pension, but they have money through Social Security and have saved $2 million. There is a big psychological difference between knowing you're going to get paid $5,000 every single month, as in the first example, and having $2 million that could *potentially* pay $5,000 every single month. There is a big difference in what people can dream about doing in retirement when they have assets that generate income. When someone comes in with guaranteed income, they can plan how they are going to live their life because they don't have to worry about running out of money. When someone has money but it is not set up as a guaranteed income stream, they plan retirement based on the fear of running out of money.

In both examples, the same investments will do the same thing—provide a renewable source of income—but one is done by the company pension plan and the other must be done by managing the savings. The first couple in this example is going through retirement with confidence because they believe their income is going to be there every single month. It's my job to recreate that for the second couple; it's my job to help them see their $2 million as a renewable income source, not a limited resource.

Let me give you another example. A couple came to see me to go through the RRR process. Like the second couple I just mentioned, this couple had $2 million in savings. They were both about to retire and didn't know what they would do in retirement. In fact, they had not really thought about retirement at all. For so long, they had focused solely on saving all that they could. After a couple of minutes of talking with them and taking notes, I realized that they had not spent any time dreaming about what they wanted to do in retirement. I put my pen down and, instead, asked each of them to take a few moments to write down three things they wanted to do when they retired. They could list things they wanted to do together or independently of each other, and I wanted them to be very specific. They both looked at me, a bit confused, and admitted that they had never thought about this before.

"Okay," I told them. "Let's have some fun. Let's start to dream." We soon discovered that they wanted to travel to the Galapagos Islands together. And the more we talked about traveling, the more they talked about how much they would like to do multiple trips each year to see places and wonders that they had never been able to visit when they were working. Before long, I was no longer even part of the conversation, and they were talking to each other about where they wanted to go. The more they talked, the more the list grew until there were twenty-five different items on it. Beyond travel, they also wanted to support their children and grandchildren, not so much by giving them money but just by being present in their lives. There were other things on their list as well, such as volunteering, learning to eat better, and taking better care of themselves physically.

At the end of our session, reality hit, and they asked me the same questions that had brought them to my office in the first place. "Can we afford to do this? How do we pay for all this?" That's when I shared with them the equation TR = I + G. We did some calculations and estimates about how often they wanted to travel, how often they wanted to be with their children and grandchildren, and what these things might cost. The estimate came to approximately $150,000 a year, which made sense to them because, when they were working, they were earning approximately the same amount.

The question then was, "How do we know we can take money out of our account to pay for this?" Well, we knew they had $5,000 a month from Social Security that would be starting shortly. That gave them $60,000 in passive income, which meant they had to come up with $90,000 from investments with their $2 million.

This is where understanding the equation TR = I + G becomes important. They now had to understand the purpose of their money. Was the purpose of their money to try to make the $2 million into $4 million? Were they trying to win the game of life again? Or was the purpose of their money to pay them the $90,000 a year for the rest of their retirement? For this couple, the decision was easy: They wanted the money to pay them for the rest of their retirement. This meant they needed to change how they invested to be income-focused first and growth-focused second. It wasn't giving up; it was about determining the best way to ensure that income would always be there.

This led to a discussion about how we needed to look at ways for their investments to bring them more than 5 percent per year in interest and dividends. This particular couple chose a more conservative path, which included very few traditional stock market investments, even though there was a whole universe of those that they could have chosen from.

We set them up to generate $110,000 a year in interest and dividends on their $2 million. Since they are living their dream retirement on $90,000 per year, then $20,000 is actually going back into the pot to generate future income. Because their income needs are naturally going to go up over time, it's necessary to reinvest that income to generate future income.

Now, this couple is no longer wondering whether they can live the retirement of their dreams; they are able to actually live it because they can see where their income is going to come from year in and year out, and market conditions will have little effect on their income. Just like previous generations had a pension that they could rely on and spend each month, this couple is now generating their own pension.

But the way we have them set up is even better because, with an actual pension, something like an unforeseen expense may require the retiree to dip into their principal. While market conditions may affect the value of this couple's investments, the income produced isn't directly tied to the investment value, so it will continue to fund their dreams.

A "Probably Will Work" Strategy?

One way to potentially undermine retirement dreams is to rely on the 4 percent rule as your strategy. The rule states that you'll succeed in retirement as long as you don't withdraw more than 4 percent annually from your retirement savings. It's based on the idea that, if you're invested for growth, you could earn more than 4 percent on your savings over the long term, so you should be able to safely withdraw 4 percent of your account per year and never run out of money. If the 4 percent you're withdrawing comes from interest and dividends, then no worries. But what if the market doesn't continue to grow by 4 percent or more, so it doesn't increase your savings and, therefore, doesn't support that 4 percent withdrawal rate—yet you keep spending the 4 percent? If the 4 percent comes from 1 percent interest and dividends and 3 percent growth but there's no growth, then you'll have to begin spending the principal. If you cannibalize your principal, then you run the risk of shattering your retirement dreams.

If you use the 4 percent rule, there are three ways it might go: (1) You might fund your retirement and win the game of life a second time, (2) you might just fund your retirement, or (3) you might run out of money before you die. The 4 percent rule is a "probably" strategy—it probably will work. But do you want "probably" as a retirement plan? Whereas, if you invest for predictable and repeatable income, then you'll live the retirement of your dreams. It's your choice.

Oranges and Crossword Puzzles

Another couple came into my office knowing they had enough money to retire. They understood the investing-for-income message right away. Everything made sense to them. Then I asked them about what they envisioned for their retirement. They said they had some simple travel plans, and they really wanted a second home someplace warmer where they could go during the winter months. They wanted to be snowbirds, but they were concerned about their expectations.

Since we knew they had the income, we came up with a plan for them to rent in several places in Florida to try out their idea before buying. Even though renting may be more expensive than buying something permanent, just talking through the idea and putting some numbers to it gave them peace of mind to know that they were making the right decision. So they needed a little bit of extra income to navigate this portion of their retirement, but the rest of their dream wasn't elaborate at all. It wasn't Instagram-worthy. They just wanted to be together where it was warmer, get up every morning, go out for a walk, buy a newspaper, pick oranges from the neighborhood trees, go home and squeeze those oranges, and then do the crossword puzzle together. They did not need first-class, around-the-world travel. They just wanted to enjoy fresh-squeezed orange juice and each other's company.

It was a different dream, but they, too, wanted their money to be safe and there for them if they needed it and to know that it would pass on to their children. They spent many years together doing the morning crossword puzzle and drinking fresh-squeezed orange juice.

Reality Check

Many times when people are discussing retirement and retirement planning with me, we have to make sure expectations and reality meet. This was an eye-opener for a single gentleman named David. He had a daughter and a grandchild, but they were doing fine without any financial help from him.

David had worked in the engineering and construction business for most of his career. All that time, he had been earning $150,000 a year, but he told me he never spent the money and that all he would need in retirement was Social Security, which would pay him $45,000 per year. He believed that he was going to retire from a $150,000-a-year job and live on $45,000 a year in retirement. That, of course, immediately raised red flags for me, but David was insistent. He said there was no reason he would need to spend more than that in retirement. David would be turning sixty-five years old, would start paying for Medicare for health insurance, and would be claiming Social Security.

I asked him a few questions about what he spent his money on, and he replied, "Not really anything." So then I started asking him some more questions about spending and we did a quick analysis, jotting down his answers on the back of an envelope before switching to my whiteboard. Doing the math, we broke down his expenses out of the $150,000. He maxed out his 401(k) to a total of $30,000 per year. He paid FICA tax on his income, which was $10,000. He had a small home equity line of credit that cost him about $1,000 a month, but it would end when he retired, so that was another $12,000 that he was spending while he was working that he would not be spending in retirement. He had $1,000 extra per month routed directly into his savings account. Altogether, that left $86,000, which was his actual spending on daily living.

David and I then sat down and had a frank discussion about what he was actually spending money on. I pushed him to confirm he wasn't saving on anything else and that there wasn't any extra money in his checking account at the end of the month. He told me there was nothing else and that he truly believed that Social Security would be more than enough for him to live on. Once we illustrated on the whiteboard that he was really spending about $86,000 a year, he realized that what he thought he could live on in retirement was not reality. He admitted that he wanted to continue his lifestyle and not live a lesser one in retirement, so he realized that he was going to need more money from day one.

Now, of course, David had his 401(k), and if he took that money and invested it for income, he would be able to make up the additional $41,000 a year that he would need to continue to lead the same lifestyle. But it was an eye-opening conversation for him to have someone show him what he was actually spending. He didn't need help determining what he was going to do in retirement; he had his plans all set—his math was just off!

It's difficult to do an analysis and realize what you're truly spending money on. Often, people just open up the checkbook, count up their expenses, make a small estimate, and assume that's what they're spending. But there are always other items that need to be figured. There are always things that happen one month and not the next, or in one quarter or one year but not the next. People often underestimate how much they are actually spending. That's why a top-down analysis is a more accurate way of factoring in all those expenses that are sometimes missed when just adding up what's in the checkbook.

A short discussion about future income also led David to believe that greater future income would be needed just because of inflation and the cost of living. It's not always about figuring out what you're going to spend your money on; it's often about making sure all the numbers line up properly.

If you are close to retirement, I would actively encourage you to sit down and dream about it. Write down what you want your retirement to be like—in the short term, the medium term, and the long term. Be specific. Dream about what you want to do as a couple, as an individual, as a family. How do you want all those pieces to fit together? What does that look like?

Ask Yourself ...

1. What is my dream for retirement?

2. How much am I currently spending each year?

3. What do I expect my income to be in retirement?

CHAPTER 3

A Fiduciary and More in Your Corner

I t's commonly believed that when someone is working on Wall Street, they're helping people make money. But when I was trading options on the floor of the Philadelphia Stock Exchange, that was not my job at all. I had a responsibility to myself and no one else, and I did what I thought was best to earn money. No one was asking me for advice. A backer gave me a big pot of money and said, "Go, trade." My only legal responsibility as a seat holder on the Philadelphia Stock Exchange was to provide liquidity in the markets for the public. I didn't have to care about what the public wanted to do; I just needed to do the opposite at a price that I determined. Every trade has two sides: Someone is buying, and someone is selling. If you want to buy a stock for $50, someone must be willing to sell it for $50, and vice versa. I had to be the other side of the trade, the opposite. It didn't matter if it was a good trade or a bad trade for the customer. If someone wanted to sell, I was there to buy; if they wanted to buy, I was there to sell—but I would pick the price.

There are too many details and intricacies involved in options trading to share all of them in this space, but here are some brief examples: Let's say the public wanted to sell at $1.25 per option and I was only willing to pay $1.15 per option. Well, I didn't have to buy the options at $1.25; I was required to buy them at $1.15. So, if a public order came in that told me to remove the $1.25 price and go ahead and sell at $1.15, I would buy the options. Then, I would trade against those options in some way. I might sell some of the underlying stock against the options I just bought, or I might buy stock against them. If I were lucky, I would be able to sell another option that was similar or even the same option to someone who wanted to buy it. If I could find that person and sell for $1.20, then I just made a nickel. If, for example, IBM stock was trading at $50 per share in July, that would be a "July 50 call." The owner of the July 50 call then has the right, but not the obligation, to buy stock at $50 per share. Just like making a reservation at a restaurant, you have the right but not the obligation to go to that restaurant. In the stock example, there is a price for that right—let's say $1. Over the course of, say, a week, if the stock price goes from $50 to $55, the right to buy the stock at $50 is very valuable because the stock that was bought for $50 could then be sold on the New York Stock Exchange for $55. Taking into account the $1 price for the right, this would mean a $4 profit: It was bought for $50, a dollar was paid for that right, and then it was sold for $55, leaving a $4 gain.

Options can also be traded. In my role, I might buy an option for $0.75 and then offer it for sale at $1.25. If someone wanted to buy it at $1.15, I might say, "No, I'll sell it for $1," and then eventually one of us would have to break. Either the buyer would pay $1.25 or the seller would settle for $1.15. That decision is based on whether the stock goes up or down; if it goes down to $45 very quickly, then the right to buy it at $50 is worthless, so it's more likely that the seller will sell. If the stock goes up, then the seller is going to want more.

Again, there are a lot more details to that role as a market maker on the Philadelphia Stock Exchange, but what's important is that, in that role, I had no fiduciary responsibility; no one on the stock exchange does. I had a legal obligation to make a liquid market, but that was it.

These days, I no longer have a responsibility to only myself. Now, I have a responsibility to help each of my clients manage their assets for income throughout retirement. That's what it means to be a fiduciary. Sure, I'm governed by the rules set forth by the SEC, but my primary concern is doing whatever is in my clients' best interests because that's the person I am.

When I first sat down with Jerry Poole, my partner who helped me get into this industry, he talked to me about what it meant to be a fiduciary and about what it meant to do the right thing. He said, "It's actually very easy; if you won't be able to defend your recommendation in front of a judge or wouldn't recommend something for your mother, then don't recommend it for someone else." That made sense to me, and it's how I live my life. I love what I do, and I view every single person's situation as different—there are no one-size-fits-all situations.

Suitability Versus Fiduciary Standard

In the financial services industry, there are, broadly speaking, two different kinds of advisors. The first is the commission-based broker, and the second is the fee-based advisor. The broker is really just a salesperson, not an advisor. The broker is held to what's known as a suitability standard. Essentially, all they have to do is recommend something suitable for you. As long as it kind of meets your goals, that's just fine. The fee-based advisor is held to what is called a fiduciary standard. This advisor must choose investments that they believe are the best recommendation for your goals. This is a legal responsibility.

Now, practically speaking, many people who call themselves advisors actually act in both capacities. The problem is transparency. Sometimes, people don't know when their advisor is acting in a fiduciary capacity or in a suitability capacity. Let me give you a quick example of a suitability standard. Remember the answer to all your retirement concerns: $TR = I + G$. If your goal is to make your money last the rest of your life, as I've been explaining, as long as you withdraw from the interest and dividends that your money earns, you should be able to achieve that goal. But if your advisor is providing income in retirement to you from the growth in the market—which no one can predict, and we have seen long periods where there is zero growth in the market—that is a suitable suggestion and OK according to the law. But there's a distinct possibility that this withdrawal method means you could run out of money before you run out of life because, without growth, you will begin to withdraw from your principal.

Imagine if we phrased this differently: "Hey, Mr. and Mrs. Client. We're going to make some assumptions and hope the stock market grows so you can live the retirement of your dreams. There's a 90 percent chance our computer model here says it'll work out, but there's a 10 percent chance that you're going to run out of money or have to seriously reduce your lifestyle in retirement." The government says that's OK, that it's suitable. I say that's ridiculous. The regulators in this industry consider an eighty-five-year-old with most of their money in the stock market just as suitable as an eighty-five-year-old holding long-term bonds that definitely will never mature until after they're deceased. Both of these are considered to be suitable investments for an eighty-five-year-old.

What's even worse about the suitability standard is that the advisor has to be licensed with a broker. And the brokerage firm that they work for is the one they have a contract with. Think about what that means. If a broker has two choices to make in an investment that's suitable for you, and one of them pays him and his firm more than the other, guess what? That's the one the advisor is going to be purchasing from. Remember that the broker has a primary obligation to his brokerage firm, not to the customer. And when you, as the customer, ask the advisor, "Hey, does this really make sense? Is this the best investment for me?" that broker can truthfully say, "Yes, it's suitable for you." That's treating you more like a retail customer and selling you a retail product instead of treating you like a client, understanding your goals, and then developing a portfolio to meet those goals. There are also discount brokers who just openly say, "We are here to help you if you already know what you're doing." At least they're not lying to you!

An SEC registered investment advisor (RIA) is a fee-only advisor who is registered with the SEC or a securities administrator in the state where they practice. The RIA that I am a part of is Sound Income Strategies, and, as part of Sound Income Strategies, I am officially titled an investment advisor representative (IAR). As an IAR, I must know you fully and truly understand you and your goals because the law requires me and Sound Income Strategies to do *what is in your best interest*, not what is suitable for you.

Let's say I'm going to sell you a life insurance policy; if I can't find the best policy for you because there are thousands of policies, then I have to do the best I can to find the life insurance that's best for you. The gray area is when I come across two policies that are very suitable for you, but one pays me more than the other; in theory, I can't do that. As a fiduciary, I have to find the best for you. That's why, in insurance, there is no fiduciary standard because there are so many options that it's impossible to find the best.

When you work with me, or any IAR at Sound Income Strategies, you now have an advisor who has been educated, trained, and licensed to talk with you about your finances and all of the options that are available to you. Not just some of the suitable ones but all of the options. This is why I have to go through a process with every single client I work with.

As a fiduciary IAR trying to generate income for retirement from your portfolio, I have a responsibility to do the best thing for you when buying and selling stocks and bonds. If someone comes in and wants to buy a mutual fund with large-cap growth stocks, well, there are a lot of mutual funds out there, and some of them will pay me a bigger finder's fee than others. As a fiduciary, I would never sell you a mutual fund because there are so many; who really knows which is the best? Now, some fiduciaries do sell mutual funds, but they're not collecting a commission for selling them; they're collecting a fee for managing them. If the mutual fund pays me, I'm acting under the suitability standard. If I sell you mutual funds and those mutual funds don't pay me a dime, but you pay me, now I'm acting under the fiduciary standard because I talked to you and said, "Hey, these are the usual ones that make sense," and you said, "Oh, yes, I agree."

The Retirement Risk Report

The process we use to help discover what is best for you is known as the Retirement Risk Report. Let me explain it in more detail. What this process does is put everything on one page and make it simpler to understand the full picture. We look at income *needs* versus income *wants* together. And there is a difference. We look at where your income is going to come from in retirement, whether it is contractually guaranteed or not, and whether it is predictable. We look at what tax changes might mean for your income. We look at the risk you are taking and whether it matches the risk that you think you should be taking. All these things are discussed during the fiduciary process that ultimately generates our one-page RRR. This brings up any red flags that might require attention. It also potentially brings up green flags to indicate where you're doing a good job. But together, we're going to understand what you know, and hopefully educate you on what you don't know. And it starts with the RRR to understand where you are right now. This helps you better move to where you want to be in the future.

During the RRR process, there are a few things that we really focus on. We start by asking questions such as the following (but the questions are actually determined by each answer):

- What is the purpose of your money? Up to now, the primary purpose of your money has just been to make it bigger. That usually changes as you get closer to retirement.

- What are your retirement investment goals?

- Why do you have these goals?

- How much money do you actually have, and can you meet those goals?

- Are the investments you have today supporting those goals, or are they hurting them?

Ultimately, the RRR will help you determine whether you are invested properly for your phase in life. If you're not, then you'll be able to make an informed change.

SOUND INCOME STRATEGIES: RETIREMENT RISK REPORT

Last Name: Smith	First Name 1: John (70)	First Name 2: Jane (68)

RANK MOST IMPORTANT TO YOU		RANK
Generate enough income to meet or exceed retirement goals		1
Make sure your risk is appropriate for you		2
Maximize growth for a large purchase		3

CURRENT DIVERSIFICATION - ACCORDING TO TAX		
Tax Deferred Account:	$1,974,605	**Initial RMD: $72,073**
Tax Free Account:	$106,665	
Taxable Account:	$0	
Total Assets:	**$2,081,270**	

CURRENT DIVERSIFICATION - ACCORDING TO INVESTMENT TYPE	
Direct Contract:	$463,627
Indirect Contract:	$568,628
No Contract (Stocks):	$1,030,715
No Contract (Other):	$0
Total Assets:	**$2,081,270**

INCOME GOALS		
	I Need	**I Want**
Expenses	$98,600	$140,000
Effective Tax Rate	17%	17%
Pretax Expenses	**$120,000**	**$170,000**

CURRENT PROJECTED INCOME SOURCES

Pension (John):	$0
Pension (Jane):	$0
SS (John):	$42,000
SS (Jane):	$30,000
Gross Investment Interest/Dividend Yield:	2.61%
Annual Fee:	0.32% (as a % of $6,657)
Net Investment Interest/Dividend Yield:	2.29%
Net Investment Interest/ Dividends:	**$47,661**
Other:	$9,000
Total Current Income:	**$128,661**

POTENTIAL PROJECTED INCOME SOURCES

Potential Current Income Yield:	5%
Potential Current Income:	**$185,064**
Additional Investment Income:	**$56,403**

MAXIMUM ACCEPTED DRAWDOWN

Max Accepted Drawdown (%):	15%
Maximum Acceptable Loss:	**$312,191**

I work with Sound Income Strategies because it has a universe of investment options available to our clients. Most people don't have a universe of investment options available to them. If your money is in a 401(k), a 403(b), the federal government Thrift Savings Plan, or a 457, then you have very limited investment options available to you. Sure, those options may be good to help you grow your money over twenty-five years when you're constantly putting money in, but are those same investment philosophies going to help you distribute your money? How do you even know? Working with a fiduciary such as any advisor at Sound Income Strategies can help you make that determination and show you that there is a whole universe of investment options available out there when your phase of life changes.

Ultimately, you have to decide whether it makes sense to hire someone to help you with this work. Whoever you hire should have a business model that fits your needs. For instance, you may have an advisor who is helping you save money and grow it during your working years, providing you with suitable investment strategies. But is that same advisor able to help you distribute your money in retirement in the most efficient and tax-efficient way?

Being a fiduciary is important. Period. Always work with a fiduciary. Not all advisors who work under the suitability standard are bad, but the suitability standard does allow for legal wiggle room that doesn't sit well with me.

Choosing a "Roofer"

In my college years, I was an assistant to someone who roofed houses— everything from typical asphalt shingles to flat roofs and slate roofs. Because of that experience, I know how to roof my own house. But let me be very clear about this: I will never roof my own house! Never mind the risk of walking around on a roof; it's not something that I would enjoy doing, and I would like to use my time differently. Could it save me money? Probably. Would that roof be suitable? I would like to think so. There are probably new technologies and techniques in the roofing industry that I'm not familiar with since the last time I installed a roof. That doesn't mean I couldn't do it, but, undoubtedly, there are professional roofers who are far better suited to the job of putting a roof on my house. What does this have to do with retirement planning? Well, let me explain through one couple's story.

Allison and Thomas came to my office to go through the RRR prompt process. Thomas was an engineer at DuPont here in Wilmington, Delaware, and for the last forty years, he had managed the couple's assets for their life together, and he had done a good job of it. He was becoming increasingly nervous about the risk that their portfolio was taking and didn't know how to invest in such a way to protect it. He was smart enough to know that some change was needed but didn't really know what that change should be.

In going through the process, we were able to discuss using a different universe of income-generating investments to help him comfortably move into retirement. As we went through the education process together, he was amazed and frankly interested in all the different kinds of investments that are out there. These are investments that he was never exposed to in his forty years of saving for retirement.

Along with this, we did a Social Security analysis and found that we could optimize their Social Security benefits as well by shifting investments to focus on income. Thomas was glad that he was able to look at the investments in front of him and know that perhaps he wasn't the person best suited to handle this phase of his life. Now, he is very smart, so in truth, he probably could have learned about all the different investment options out there and changed his investment philosophy on his own. But he decided that it really wasn't something he wanted to do himself because he didn't want to take a chance on their retirement assets. In other words, although Thomas could have done his own "roof," and it probably would have worked out, instead, he chose to do things that he really enjoys and let the professionals handle the job. Instead of trying to manage retirement income for himself and Allison, the two of them are sailing in the Chesapeake together, knowing that they've partnered with a fiduciary—Sound Income Strategies—that has their best interests at heart.

Ask Your Advisor ...

Here are some questions and answers to consider when vetting advisors to help with your retirement plan:

1. **Question**: What are your education, training, and experience?

    Answer: When it comes to financial advisors, you ideally want them to have some sort of college or postcollege finance/marketing/accounting degree.

2. **Question**: What is your basic investment philosophy?

    Answer: Not only should they be able to tell you what to invest in but also why you should choose a particular investment. Does their investment philosophy support your goals?

3. **Question**: How do you intend to get the cash I need out of my portfolio to live the retirement of my dreams?

    Answer: If they suggest selling off investment shares, such as mutual funds, rather than distributing the interest and dividends, then you should grab your wallet and run in the opposite direction as fast as possible! (Thanks to David Scranton for this great visual. It always makes me smile!)

4. **Question**: How long have you been in the financial industry and acting as a fiduciary and independent financial advisor?

   Answer: Time and experience bring knowledge.

CHAPTER 4

Same Tools, Different Build

O ften, during my RRR process, I have conversations that start off something like this:

"I now see I'm not earning enough interest and dividends from my current portfolio allocation to meet my income needs in retirement," says my client. "And I can see that generating a higher dividend or interest payment can meet those needs. I just don't see how I can do that."

"So what you're asking me," I often respond, "is how do we make the sausage? You want to see the nitty-gritty, the details, the actual execution of earning the interest in dividends you need?"

The Tools

If this sounds familiar to you, then buckle up, because here we go. This is usually the fun part for me because it's when clients start to realize that there's a whole universe of income-generating investments out there that they never knew existed. I'm going to start with the primary investments that most people could find useful.

Annuities

Annuities are complex income-generating investment tools that, if used correctly, might be appropriate for someone approaching retirement, in retirement, or looking for safety. Because of the complex nature of these investments, I will cover them separately in the next chapter. Moving on ...

Corporate Bonds and Government Bonds

There are a tremendous number of different types of corporate bonds and different bond ratings. We've all seen these ratings. There are government ratings, often AAA. Then, there are AA bonds, A bonds, BBB bonds, and so on. As you progress through the bond ratings, the risk of default on these bonds increases.

The big thing to remember about bonds is that they are contractual. A corporate bond is essentially a loan to a creditworthy company that promises two things: regular interest payments (usually twice yearly) and a return on your original investment at the end of the term. This is the maturity date at which the company will pay you back the full amount you initially invested.

Let me recap this. You sign a contract to give a certain amount of money to a company that will be repaid at a specific date in the future. Along the way, the company is also going to pay you interest payments for borrowing your money. For retirees looking for income, corporate bonds can be attractive. Why? Predictable income. You know exactly how much interest you'll receive and when. Therefore, you know exactly how much you can spend. However, the key factors of fixed-income investments, such as bonds, are interest rates, maturity, and duration. If an investment brings 5 percent and interest rates go to 8 percent, you're going to feel like you're missing out. But if a 5 percent investment ends and interest rates drop to 3 percent, you'll wish you still had that 5 percent.

It is important to remember that the guarantees bonds offer—regular interest payments and the promise to repay your original investment at maturity—are based on the company's ability to pay. If the company goes bankrupt, you may lose some or all of your investment. This is why it's crucial to consider the financial health of the company when buying corporate bonds.

This is exactly where Sound Income Strategies comes in; our precise area of knowledge is the analysis of investments such as bonds. For retirees who want a balance of income and safety, it is often recommended to invest in a mix of high-quality corporate bonds from stable companies that can provide a steady income while managing risk.

Preferred Stocks

Preferred stocks are another tool for diversifying a portfolio. They are unique investment vehicles that combine some of the features of stocks and bonds, which makes them an interesting option for those approaching or even in retirement.

Preferred stocks pay dividends, as do common stocks; however, with preferred stocks, the dividends are typically fixed and paid at regular intervals, similar to bond interest payments. Also, similar to bonds, preferred stocks are more like a loan to the company, with you, the investor, as the lender. The value of preferred stock is the value at which the company can redeem that stock in the future; they give you your money back. This is unlike common stock, where the company can offer to repurchase your stock from you for a price; as a shareholder in the company, you can continue to hold on to the stock if you choose.

One of the benefits of preferred stocks is predictable income provided by fixed dividends. It's a fixed dollar amount that you will receive so long as the company doesn't go out of business. That makes preferred stocks lower risk than common stocks because the prices are less volatile. Preferred stocks generally cost no more than common stocks, but the dividends are often higher than those paid by common stocks or interest rates. Now, the preferred stock price may go up or down, but because the dividend is a fixed dollar amount, that is what you can rely on in retirement. As a simple example, let's say a preferred stock is issued at $25, with a dividend of $1.25. No matter whether the preferred stock increases in price to $26 or lowers to $24, you will still receive the $1.25 dividend. Because of the fixed dollar amount, preferred stocks offer some inflation protection.

Also, preferred stockholders have priority over common stockholders when it comes to receiving dividends and assets. This matters should the company ultimately need to liquidate. However, there are no voting rights with a preferred stock, whereas common stocks come with voting rights and a say in company decisions.

Some preferred stocks are cumulative, meaning that if the company misses a dividend payment, it must pay the lender (the buyer of the preferred stock) before paying common stock dividends. However, preferred and common stocks both fall in line behind corporate bonds, as we saw during the COVID-19 pandemic when

Carnival Cruise Line stopped paying its preferred stock and common stock dividends but continued to pay its corporate bond debt.

Although preferred stocks are not classified as growth-oriented like common stocks, which can appreciate in value, preferred stock prices can increase if interest rates fall or the company's financial health improves. Some preferred stocks allow for dividend increases if the company's profits rise. And, as I mentioned, there are callable preferred stocks; if interest rates fall, the company might call or buy back the stock at a premium to par value. However, some preferred stocks are convertible, allowing holders to exchange them for common stock if the company performs well. These are things that the investment committee team at Sound Income Strategies looks at—whether it makes sense to convert, and when.

It is important to know that while preferred stocks can offer attractive income and some growth potential, they also come with risks. These include interest rate risk, because their value may decrease if interest rates rise, and company-specific risks. All in all, adding preferred stocks to a portfolio is a slight increase in risk but still a very good addition and essentially a baseline investment for generating income along with corporate bonds.

Business Development Companies

Business development companies (BDCs) are an interesting addition to a retirement portfolio and something we use at Sound Income Strategies, especially for those seeking predictable income. Let's break down the benefits.

A BDC is a publicly traded company that invests in small and medium-sized businesses, typically in the United States. BDCs are regulated under the Investment Company Act of 1940. Similar to mutual funds, investing in a BDC provides debt and equity capital to businesses that may have difficulty accessing traditional financing. Typically, big corporations are funded by issuing corporate bonds on Wall Street while smaller businesses operate on loans through banks. But where do companies in the middle go when they need funding? They go to a BDC.

BDCs make money through interest, loans, capital gains, and dividends from their investments. Here's why that's important for retirees: BDCs are required to distribute at least 90 percent of their taxable income to shareholders as dividends. That means the BDC can't hold back dividends from you in retirement, even if there's some unforeseen economic event. Think pandemic: During the COVID-19 pandemic, BDCs continued to pay their dividends because, under law, they had to distribute 90 percent of their taxable income to shareholders. So, as long as the loans on the debt are being paid, you know that you are going to get your dividend, and that predictability of income, as I've been saying, is critical in retirement. Also, BDCs often offer higher dividend yields, so they can provide a significant income stream for retirees.

BDCs invest in a variety of businesses across different sectors, which helps spread risk within the BDC itself. BDCs allow individual investors to gain exposure to private companies, which are usually only accessible to higher-dollar institutional investors. At Sound Income Strategies, we do the research to allow you to know which BDC has the potential to be better.

While income is the primary focus of investing in BDCs, they can also experience share price growth, or appreciation, especially if their investments perform well. In addition, there is a tremendous amount of transparency because, as traded companies, BDCs must provide regular financial reports. They are managed by professionals who handle the complexities of lending and investing in private business.

Everything we're talking about with BDCs really comes down to the predictability of income in retirement. Let's zero in on that again. The requirement to distribute 90 percent of taxable income leads to regular, predictable dividend payouts. There's a stable business model because BDCs typically focus on generating steady income through interest and dividends from their investments rather than relying on capital gains. There are diversified income streams because BDCs invest in multiple businesses. BDCs often have floating loans to help maintain income levels even in rising interest rate environments, which helps lower your interest rate risk. Again, the quarterly distributions often align with retirees' income needs, and many established BDCs have a history of maintaining consistent dividend payments, which can be reassuring for retirees planning for their retirement income.

It's important to note that while BDCs can offer attractive income potential, they also come with risks that include exposure to business sensitivity, economic cycles, and share price volatility. This is why it's important to understand how BDCs work and why they represent a portion of what we invest in for our clients at Sound Income Strategies. But they are only one of the types of investments that we use.

Real Estate Investment Trusts

Real estate investment trusts (REITs) are a popular choice for those approaching or in retirement because of their potential for providing steady income. Let's explore how they work and why they can be beneficial.

REITs are companies that own, operate, or finance income-producing real estate. There are equity REITs (which manage properties), mortgage REITs (which finance real estate), and hybrid REITs (which do both). They generate income through rent, property appreciation, and sometimes interest on adjustable-rate mortgages. REITs must distribute at least 90 percent of their taxable income to shareholders annually as dividends, making them attractive for individual investors.

REITs can enhance retirement portfolios because they offer higher dividend yields compared to many stocks, providing a significant income stream. They provide regular, consistent payments, often quarterly, aligning well with retirees' needs for steady income. They also offer exposure to real estate without the need to manage properties directly, investing across various real estate types, such as office, retail, residential, and healthcare.

REITs are professionally managed, removing the need for investors to have knowledge of property management. While income is their primary focus, REIT share prices can appreciate, offering some growth potential. They also act as an inflation hedge since real estate values and rents tend to rise with inflation. Since they are publicly traded, REITs offer the liquidity of stocks, allowing for easy buying and selling.

For retirees, REITs provide a steady stream of rental income and help manage cash flow with quarterly distributions. Many REITs have a history of maintaining or growing dividend payments over time, providing reassurance for retirement planning. Additionally, sectors such as healthcare or storage units tend to be less cyclical, potentially offering more stable income through economic ups and downs.

Dividend Stocks

Dividend stocks can be an excellent addition to a retirement portfolio, offering the best of both worlds: income and potential growth. These are sometimes called common stocks, which are the stocks everyone thinks about when talking about the stock market. But what I'm actually talking about in this section is a subset of common stocks. Let's take a quick dive into how dividend stocks work.

The best way to start is with the definition. Dividend stocks are shares through which companies regularly distribute a portion of their earnings to shareholders, typically quarterly. The annual dividend payment, known as a dividend yield, is expressed as a percentage of the stock's current price. The company decides on dividend amounts based on its earnings, cash flow, and growth plans. Many companies aim to increase dividends over time as their earnings grow. Hopefully, there will be dividend growth! There's potential for reinvestment in the company because investors can choose to receive dividends or cash, or reinvest these to buy more shares.

For an income investor and retiree, dividend stocks can be good for a retirement portfolio. For starters, dividends provide a steady stream of income, which is crucial, of course, for retirees, and payments are typically made quarterly, aligning well with ongoing living expenses. There is potential for income growth because many companies potentially increase dividends over time to offset inflation; this can lead to growing income for retirees, even without selling shares. Since, as we all know, life gets more expensive, you need your income to grow. While we're always income-focused at Sound Income Strategies, we don't want to ignore the potential for growth, and again, dividend stocks can offer both. This combination can help maintain purchasing power over the long term. Dividend stocks also have lower volatility than the stock market in general because dividend-paying companies are often more established and stable, potentially leading to less price volatility. There is some flexibility with dividend stocks because investors can choose to reinvest dividends during the accumulation years and then switch to taking cash payments in retirement. And of course, diversification within dividend-paying stocks is available across sectors, allowing for diversification in a portfolio.

Many dividend-paying companies have a long history of regular dividend payments. Some dividend aristocrats have increased their dividends annually for at least twenty-five consecutive years. Wow! Isn't that what we're all looking for? Quarterly payments provide regular predictable income streams because there is a strong commitment to shareholders. Moreover, companies that pay dividends often prioritize these accounts, maintaining or growing payments because cuts can negatively impact stock prices. There's tremendous transparency because dividend amounts and payment dates are announced in advance, allowing for better financial planning. There's also some sector stability because sectors such as utilities, consumer staples, and healthcare are known for stable dividends even during economic downturns. This is important because we want to know that we're going to be paid regardless of the economic situation.

It is important to know that although dividend stocks can offer attractive income potential, they also come with risks. These include the possibility of dividend cuts during economic hardship, company-specific risks, and general market volatility. Dividends may not be sustainable in the long run, so it's crucial to look beyond just the yield. There is no easy mutual fund at Vanguard, Fidelity, Schwab, or anywhere else with a super-safe, high 5 or 6 percent dividend payment.

Generating reliable retirement income doesn't mean you're limited to the stock market. While many people associate contractual income solely with annuities and certificates of deposit (CDs), there's actually a wide range of income-producing investments available. These include bonds, preferred stocks, high-quality dividend stocks, REITs, and BDCs.

Although these investments may experience market volatility, it doesn't necessarily affect their income payments. The key to retirement planning isn't just about maximizing your final net worth—it's about creating dependable income streams that outpace inflation.

While we'd all like guaranteed 10 percent yields with perfect safety, that's not realistic in today's investment world. However, we can build portfolios that generate reliable retirement income without depending solely on stock market appreciation. The goal is to create steady income while maintaining principal protection through diversification and careful security selection.

Our experienced portfolio management team can help develop an income strategy tailored to your needs. Please feel free to contact me directly or reach out to Carla in our office to discuss your retirement income goals.

Other Tools

There are some other tools that you can potentially use that I will not cover in too much depth here, but they include CDs from banks, US treasuries (federally issued bonds), and municipal bonds (any government bond that's not federal). Generally speaking, I do not like to use pooled investment vehicles—these are investments where your funds are pooled together, either with multiple investors for a common objective or with funds from many investors to create a portfolio (as in the case of a mutual fund).

Investing for Income

After someone goes through my RRR process and decides that it makes sense to shift their investment focus and be advised by me and my expert team at Sound Income Strategies, then I go through an education process with them. I call this education process I4I, or Investing for Income. During the process, I walk through all the different types of investments that you might want to include in your income portfolio, and it's always an interesting exercise. The I4I process that most sticks out in my mind is the one I went through with a gentleman named Terry.

Terry was never married, had no children, and, generally speaking, had managed his own investments for his entire life. He had recently retired, and we were rolling his 401(k) into an IRA and making the shift to income strategies. I went through my process of educating him on the different investment options available to him in the income-generating world. Terry always asked a lot of questions, and this meeting was no different. As I went through each of the investments, we had detailed discussions about how they worked and whether it made sense to have them in his portfolio. When we were finished talking through them, we made an allocation decision that was customized to Terry. He was happy with the process and the decisions that we'd made. Then I asked him whether he had any final questions or wanted to know the details about anything else. He told me that he thought he understood everything well and was happy with the decisions. Then he paused for a moment before asking, "James, why has no one ever explained this to me before? I've been investing with large institutions that provide support phone numbers and people to speak to, and no one's ever said anything about these investments that we're looking at. It's always mutual funds, mutual funds, mutual funds, which you don't really like. Why is it that, in over forty years of investing and talking with the help reps at big companies, no one ever explained these investments to me and certainly didn't explain any investment to me in the depth that we just covered?"

I thought about Terry's question for a moment and then said, "Terry, I don't know. I wish it was talked about more. This is why Sound Income Strategies was formed in the first place."

Although that was the answer I gave Terry, there is a reason why the details of these investments that I just shared with you are never covered by the big companies. It's something my team and I call "the disease of ease." You see, mutual funds are easy. You just check a box on the page of your investment portfolio. You don't have to do any intense research. You don't have to pick any stocks. Someone else is doing all that for you. It's easy for you, but the reason there isn't a super-safe mutual fund that pays 5 or 6 percent in interest and dividends is because it's really just not that easy. The amount of research and effort that goes into developing a customized portfolio for our clients is difficult. So when a big brokerage shop wants to hire people to sell their investment products, they often take the easy way; they just buy mutual funds where someone else is doing the work and are paid a fee. It is the easy way out, but I learned a long time ago that the easy way out is rarely the best way.

Teach Yourself Predictable Income Options ...

- **Corporate bonds and government bonds** are contractual options that have different ratings. They are loans.

- **Preferred stocks** pay dividends at fixed and regular intervals; often, the dividends are higher than those paid by common stocks or interest rates. Similar to bonds, they are more like a loan to a company.

- **BDCs** are publicly traded companies that invest in small and medium-sized businesses, typically in the US.

- **REITs** own, operate, or finance income-producing real estate across various sectors, and they must distribute at least 90 percent of their taxable income to shareholders annually in the form of dividends.

- **Dividend stocks** offer income and potential growth. These are shares through which companies regularly pay dividends.

- **Other tools** include CDs from banks, US treasuries (federally issued bonds), and municipal bonds (any government bond that's not federal).

CHAPTER 5

Annuities

A nnuities can help retirees generate income or provide safety in retirement. They often spark strong opinions, but like any investment, annuities have pros and cons. They're neither universally perfect nor useless; their suitability depends on individual needs.

Unlike other investments, annuities are often aggressively sold, contributing to their polarizing reputation. However, annuities are simply another tool for generating income and protecting assets. I don't "sell" annuities more than I do other investments. Instead, I guide clients through options to find what fits them best.

Take Eric, who valued safety for his retirement assets. He chose an annuity after being educated about various options. The decision was his, based on his comfort with the annuity's benefits.

Many clients decide against annuities, which is also fine. The key is informed choice without pressure. Annuities should be one of many tools considered for retirement income.

Let's explore the different types of annuities. Most allow you to assign a beneficiary and adjust investment amounts. Standard annuity contracts have no fees, but additional riders offer extra benefits at a cost. Payments start when you decide and continue as long as the terms and riders allow.

Annuities can be a valuable part of your retirement strategy, but always ensure they fit your specific needs.

Fixed Annuities

Fixed annuities are similar to bank CDs but are longer term, making them more suitable for retirement planning. They're contracts with insurance companies and offer a stated interest rate for a set period. Unlike CDs, which are FDIC-insured, fixed annuities are backed by the insurance company's investments, often in corporate bonds, which can offer higher rates and potentially lower default risks.

Banks lend to individuals, while insurance companies invest in corporate bonds, making insurance companies generally more stable. Most states have guaranteed funds to protect against insurance company failures, similar to the FDIC.

Fixed annuities have no fees but may have surrender charges for early withdrawals. These charges decrease over time, typically allowing 10 percent annual withdrawals without penalty. After the surrender period, you can access your funds without additional charges.

Understanding these aspects can help you decide whether fixed annuities fit your retirement strategy.

Fixed Index Annuities

Fixed index annuities are a type of fixed annuity with protection against loss, but their interest rate depends on the performance of an external index, such as the S&P 500. If the market drops, you don't lose money, but you earn 0 percent interest. If the market rises, you gain a portion of the increase, which is determined by a cap or participation rate.

For example, with a 9 percent cap, if the market gains 5 percent, you get 5 percent, but if it gains 12 percent, you only get 9 percent. With a 50 percent participation rate, a 5 percent market gain results in 2.5 percent interest, and a 20 percent gain gives you 10 percent.

Fixed index annuities are popular because they offer growth potential with some level of protection. Riders can be added to provide lifetime income and leave the remaining principal to your heirs.

Immediate Annuities

With an immediate annuity, you give a lump sum to an insurance company in exchange for lifetime payments, essentially buying a pension. You get a guaranteed monthly income for life, but you no longer have access to the lump sum. The payments are based on the lump sum given, your age, and interest rates, with the insurance company determining the payout based on life expectancy. If you outlive this expectancy, you benefit; if not, the insurance company keeps the remaining funds. Your heirs don't receive any portion upon your death.

Immediate annuities offer the highest monthly payments but at the cost of beneficiary benefits. They're a useful tool for maximizing monthly income, and though I rarely recommend them, it's essential to be aware of this option.

Variable Annuities

Variable annuities are often criticized for their high fees and complexity. They have subaccounts similar to mutual funds, each with its own management fees, and a mortality and expense (M&E) charge, typically totaling over 2 percent. Unlike other annuities, variable annuities involve market risk and can lose value. Brokers might add income protection riders, raising the total fees to 3–4 percent or more.

This high fee structure combined with market volatility can significantly deplete your principal, especially when drawing income. Fixed annuities and other annuities typically have no fees or much lower fees, making them more stable options.

Understanding the nuances of different annuity types is crucial. While variable annuities often give all annuities a bad name, it's important to know that other annuities can be safer and more cost-effective. Always educate yourself and make informed decisions about your investments.

Know the Different Kinds of Annuities ...

FIXED ANNUITIES

- earn a stated rate of interest each year;

- apply surrender charges for a stated period of time;

- usually allow for 10 percent liquidity with no penalty;

- incur no fees;

- offer the ability to add a lifetime income rider for a fee, if desired; and

- offer additional insurance protection from the state they are issued in.

FIXED INDEXED ANNUITIES

- earn an interest rate based on the performance of a market index;

- offer potential for greater interest over fixed annuities;

- offer potential for 0 percent interest years;

- apply surrender charges for a stated period of time;

- usually allow for 10 percent liquidity with no penalty;

- incur no fees;

- offer the ability to add a lifetime income rider for a fee, if desired; and

- offer additional insurance protection from the state they are issued in.

IMMEDIATE ANNUITIES

- involve you irrevocably giving a lump sum of money to the insurance company;

- provide you with a lifetime income stream;

- incur no fees;

- provide no death benefits to beneficiaries; and

- provide you with the highest monthly income.

VARIABLE ANNUITIES
(JUST DON'T DO THIS EVER!)

- invest assets in subaccounts with market risk;

- charge an M&E fee/subaccount fee/income guarantee fee (generally 3–5 percent annually!);

- have the potential for greater interest over fixed annuities (if you get really lucky!);

- apply surrender charges for a stated period of time; and

- usually allow for 10 percent liquidity with no penalty.

CHAPTER 6

Social Security

Without Social Security benefits, 38.7 percent of older adults would have incomes below the federal poverty level; all else being equal, with Social Security benefits, only 10.2 percent do. The benefits lift an estimated 16.5 million older adults above the federal poverty level.[1]

If you have taken the effort to read this book, you are not part of the 38.7 percent who will have incomes below the federal poverty level. I started out this chapter with that statistic because it shows just how important Social Security is for helping Americans. But for our purposes and discussions, Social Security is just another tool in the toolbox; it's going to provide income just like dividend stocks, bonds, or an annuity.

I offer many Social Security educational workshops both in person and through webinars, and the consistent question I hear is "When should I start my Social Security?" Here's the answer: It

---

1   Kathleen Romig, *Social Security Lifts More People Above the Poverty Line Than Any Other Program* (Washington, DC: Center on Budget and Policy Priorities, last modified January 21, 2025), https://www.cbpp.org/research/social-security/social-security-lifts-more-people-above-the-poverty-line-than-any-other.

depends. If we just look at it in terms of math, there's only one right way to start taking Social Security: Start your Social Security at age seventy and live to age eighty-two. This will maximize the amount you will extract from the Social Security system. Now, of course, we can't guarantee we're going to live to eighty-two, and sometimes there's more to it than just trying to die with the most money we can. What if you're in your midsixties and have just been let go from your job and can't afford to wait until you're seventy? Go ahead and start your Social Security. It's OK. Don't let someone tell you that you're throwing away money. You're not. You're living your life. What if you are not healthy and you don't think you're going to live to eighty-two? Well, it might be a good idea to file before your full retirement age (FRA).

I use a proprietary software tool to help assess when it might be best to begin Social Security. There are some inputs that go into the tool, such as a person's life expectancy and need for the money. Without making a proper analysis, there's a distinct possibility you could be leaving thousands of dollars on the table unclaimed.

During my Social Security workshops, I often show examples of how people could extract more from the Social Security system just by applying the right way. For instance, I had a couple come in to walk through my RRR process after going through my Social Security educational workshop. During the process, we also ran our Social Security analysis software. Initially, they were all set on how they were going to apply for Social Security. They had both planned on starting their Social Security right at their FRA. After running the analysis, we found out that one could apply a little bit early and the other a little bit later than FRA. This would result in them earning $52,000 extra over their lifetimes. In this couple's case, coming to the workshop and sitting down to be educated through the RRR process was worth $52,000. Needless to say, they were happy.

I tell this simple story because many people make an assessment on when to apply for Social Security based on things that seem strange to me: *This is when my neighbor applied; this is when my parents applied; this is when my sister applied, so I'm going to do the same thing.* You are not your neighbor, you are not your parents, and you are not your sibling. Your situation is unique.

Your Statement—What the Numbers Mean

One of the first steps to understanding your benefits is to go to the Social Security website: www.ssa.gov. There, you can create a free account and download your statement. Take a few minutes to review the statement and make sure everything looks correct. Are there any years when you filed taxes that are not reflected on your Social Security statement? After all, this is the US government we are talking about; it's not a flawless system, and mistakes are often made.

Next, look for a big number on the front of your statement: This is your primary insurance amount (PIA). You'll receive this PIA at your FRA. Your FRA depends on the year you were born. If you were born between 1943 and 1954, your FRA is sixty-six. The FRA gradually increases between 1955 and 1960. For anyone born in 1960 or later, the FRA is sixty-seven.

Even though your FRA is a set number, according to the Social Security Administration, you can begin Social Security benefits earlier or later than that full retirement date. If your FRA is sixty-seven and you decide to begin benefits at age sixty-two—which is the earliest you can start—you will receive 70 percent of what your FRA benefit would be. For example, if your PIA is $1,000 a month when you reach sixty-seven but you go ahead and start Social Security at sixty-two, then you would receive a benefit of $700. If you decide to wait until age seventy, you will receive 124 percent of your PIA. (In the $1,000 example, at age seventy, the benefit would be $1,240.) This is why waiting is the best mathematical way to collect Social Security. The increased benefit will ultimately result in a larger payment if you live long enough. And today, people are living longer than ever. I see people all the time living well into their nineties. If even only one person in a couple lives into their nineties, the additional Social Security collected could easily exceed $100,000 more than if it was started early.

Will Social Security Always Be There?

I often hear people comment that they want to start Social Security early because it may not be there in the future. This implies that the government is somehow going to one day just cut off benefits. This is so far from the truth that anyone even suggesting it is trying to spread fear for the sake of fear. The Social Security trust fund is solvent. Yes, there will need to be changes and adjustments to how benefits are paid out in the future, and I would expect future collectors of Social Security to get less in some form or another. Just look at me: I'm receiving less than my parents because they were able to collect the FRA benefit at age sixty-six and I cannot collect it until I'm sixty-seven. But it's not going to just disappear.

Spousal Versus Survivor Benefits

Social Security benefits are not strictly for individuals who worked and paid into the system; they can also support family members in certain situations.

For instance, there is the spousal benefit. The spousal benefit was created because, when Social Security was started in 1935, many women stayed home raising children and maintaining a household. This is a tremendous amount of work that provides enormous benefit to our society and comes with no paycheck. From the Social Security point of view, if a couple were to apply, and a husband had a PIA of $3,000 at FRA, the spousal benefit—the wife's benefit—would be a minimum of one half of the husband's PIA. One half of $3,000 would be $1,500. This is the wife's monthly benefit, even if she never had a "paycheck" and put money into the Social Security system. The spousal benefit also applies, for example, if you were married for more than ten years and then divorced; in which case, you could file for half of your ex-spouse's PIA. Your ex-spouse would never know, and it wouldn't affect them at all. You can receive benefits on your ex-spouse's record even if they have remarried. Your ex-spouse just has to have reached age sixty-two or older, and then you can apply on their benefit.

There is also something called survivor benefits, which are often missed by those who could receive them. If you're married and your spouse passes away, you, as the surviving spouse, have a choice: You can keep your own benefit or switch over to the larger Social Security benefit of your deceased spouse. Sometimes, people are aware of this benefit, but they fail to plan for taxes because, at the same time that they switch from the smaller to the larger benefit, they also begin filing a tax return as a single, so their taxes will likely go up. There's a drop in income and an increase in taxes. When you are married for more than ten years and then divorce, you are still eligible for survivor benefits from your ex-spouse, provided you did not remarry before age sixty. If you remarry after age sixty, then the remarriage does not affect your eligibility for survivor benefits. Why is this important?

Because, in theory, survivor benefits may provide a larger amount, whereas spousal benefit is typically only about half.

More than one person can collect Social Security benefits on anyone's record. For example, if a person is deceased, and they had both a widow and an ex-spouse, both of those spouses (the widow and the ex) can collect on the deceased's benefit and it will not affect the benefit amount for either spouse.

Always remember that your benefits are your benefits, and they don't negatively or positively affect anyone else. For example, if you have a child under the age of sixteen or you're caring for a disabled child, you are also eligible for benefits on the record of your former spouse. There is no need for a ten-year length of marriage, but the child must be your former spouse's child.

Working and Collecting Social Security

Just because you're working doesn't mean you can't collect Social Security. The terms "retired" and "full retirement age" are just what the Social Security Administration uses to understand what your benefit is. If you want to keep working and collect Social Security, you can. In fact, every year you work could potentially affect the calculation that goes into collecting your Social Security and increase your Social Security benefit based on your work record.

Something to watch out for if you decide to do this is what's called the earnings test. If you are younger than your FRA and still working and you decide to collect Social Security, then your benefit will be reduced by one dollar for every two dollars earned above the annual limit. The annual limit in 2024 was $22,320 a year. If you were to earn $32,320 in a year while being younger than your FRA and you were collecting Social Security, your Social Security would be reduced by $5,000 because you are $10,000 over the earnings limit and are therefore reduced by one dollar for every two dollars earned above that limit. Once you reach FRA, your benefit is no longer reduced, regardless of how much you earn. If you continue to work, your record will be recalculated every year using the new earnings to increase your benefit. Even though the earnings test looks like a reduction of benefits, it is actually not. When you reach FRA, the Social Security Administration will recalculate your monthly benefit and credit you the amount that your benefit was reduced to because of earnings before your FRA. It takes about fifteen years before you realize the full return on that credit. So why does the Social Security Administration reduce your benefit if it's just going to give it back to you? Who knows? But now you're informed.

Reduced:

Be mindful of the earnings test if you decide to collect Social Security while still working and younger than your FRA. For every two dollars earned above the annual limit ($23,400 in 2025), your benefit reduces by one dollar. For example, earning $33,400 would reduce your Social Security by $5,000.

When you reach FRA, benefits are no longer reduced, regardless of earnings. Your record is recalculated yearly, potentially increasing your benefit. Although it seems like a benefit reduction, Social Security recalculates your benefit at FRA, crediting the amount reduced earlier. Full return on this credit takes about fifteen years.

So, while the earnings test seems confusing, it's essential to be aware of its impact on your benefits.

You should also be aware that if you are collecting Social Security before your FRA and are going to be subject to some sort of reduction, this doesn't show up until you file your taxes the following year. So, if you made too much money, not only will you have to pay taxes on the money you've earned but you'll also have to reimburse Social Security for the excess amount you received. This reimbursement is not a penalty, but it sure is going to feel like one when you have to write that check!

Taxes on Social Security

When Social Security was initially implemented by President Franklin Delano Roosevelt, it was not taxed and was never meant to be taxed. Guess what? Your Social Security is taxed today. How does that work? It gets taxed based on a calculated number called your provisional income. Provisional income is calculated by adding together half of your Social Security benefit plus any other income you receive from pensions, annuities, interest, dividends, and wages. It also includes any nontaxable municipal bond interest you're receiving. If you file as single and your provisional income is between $25,000 and $34,000, then half of your benefits could be taxed. Above $34,000, then 85 percent of your Social Security is subject to taxation. If you're filing jointly and your joint provisional income is between $32,000 and $44,000, then half of your joint Social Security is subject to taxation. For joint filers, provisional income above $44,000 means that 85 percent of your Social Security will be subject to taxation.

Social Security is complex, but it's an important tool in the income toolbox. Investigate this further on your own by going to the Social Security website (www.ssa.gov) to learn as much as you can. Talk to your financial advisor and have them explain the potential issues around Social Security and how applying may benefit you. You worked hard to earn the right to collect Social Security, so make sure you know what you can earn and how to best take advantage of it. Don't leave money on the table for the government to keep.

Educate Yourself ...

- Understand your benefit (www.ssa.gov).

- Understand when you are eligible to apply.

- Understand what factors allow you to maximize your benefit.

- Understand how your benefit is taxed.

- Trust that Social Security will be there for you.

CHAPTER 7

Roth Conversions

The RRR process is the same for everyone, but I'm always amazed at how it affects people differently and what each person takes away from the process.

For example, take Janet, a longtime client of our team. She had always been a hard worker, but retirement seemed like a distant dream to her. As a registered nurse, she loved her job but was concerned about having enough money to enjoy her later years. The RRR process changed her life.

In reviewing Janet's material during the process, it was evident she was a candidate for Roth conversions. Janet openly said that it sounded like a foreign language to her, and she laughed nervously. But once she realized that this process would allow her to withdraw money from her accounts without having to pay taxes on them, she saw the potential to have more money to spend in retirement.

Over eight years, we helped Janet convert portions of her traditional IRA assets into a Roth IRA. When Janet finally retired at age sixty-five, she was amazed at the difference those small conversions had made. She has many friends who never did Roth conversions, are now stressed about RMDs, and are often surprised by their tax bills in April. With Janet's mix of traditional and Roth accounts, she has flexibility and peace of mind with her portfolio. And with the taxes she saved by having that money in her Roth account, Janet was able to help her granddaughter with college tuition in the same year that she took a dream vacation to Italy and the Mediterranean. It's not about having some complex elaborate strategy or using big fancy words. It's about helping people such as Janet have the retirement they deserve. Janet is a testament to how a simple and small amount of financial planning and the right strategy can make retirement easy.

Traditional IRA or 401(k) Versus Roth IRA

A traditional IRA or 401(k) is money that you have saved pretax. If you earn $100,000 and put $10,000 into your IRA, when you report your income to the IRS, you will only report $90,000. The $10,000 is pretax money in the IRA or 401(k) that is allowed to grow tax-deferred. When you do eventually get to retirement, because you did not pay any taxes on this money since you put it in the account, then when you withdraw the money, it will all be taxable. You get a tax break going in, you get a tax break while it's inside the IRA or 401(k), and then you pay taxes when it comes out.

A Roth IRA is a little different. A Roth IRA is funded with after-tax dollars. It then grows tax-free, and when you withdraw the money, it will still be tax-free. A good way to think of the difference between a Roth IRA and a traditional IRA is a classic farmer analogy. With a traditional IRA, you buy the seeds without paying any taxes, but when you harvest your crop, you have to pay taxes on the whole crop. With a Roth IRA, you pay tax on the seeds when you buy them, but when you harvest the crop, it's all tax-free.

While it may seem like a good idea to always invest in a Roth IRA (and it is!), it's important to understand who should be making Roth contributions and who should be making Roth conversions. There's a slight difference between a contribution and a conversion. The contribution comes from money you are earning at your current job—you are allowed to contribute a certain amount based on your age, and taxes are paid on it when the money goes into the account. A Roth conversion is pretax money that you have saved in a different tax year, which you are now going to pay tax on before moving it into a Roth account.

Taking Taxes into Consideration

Everyone tries to diversify their investments: some stocks, some bonds; some domestic investments, some international; some conservative investments, some aggressive. The same is true of tax types. Think of tax as having three different buckets. One is the pretax bucket: This is money that you put into a traditional IRA or 401(k) to defer paying taxes on the money to a later date. The second is the tax-free bucket, which is the Roth IRA: This is money that you put in after you pay taxes on it, but you don't pay taxes on it when the money is withdrawn. The third is the taxable bucket: This is money that you have paid taxes on but put away into a vehicle that is earning interest, dividends, or capital gains on which you will pay taxes on an annual basis.

In addition to tax diversification, consider your income levels in retirement—this can help determine what you may pay in income taxes. First, do you believe you're going to have more income in retirement than you're earning now? If you've done a good job with your retirement planning, you might have more income in retirement. That's great, but it might push you into a higher tax bracket. Speaking of tax brackets, it's safe to assume that tax brackets are going to go up in the future. We're really at historic lows in regard to taxes, and we have been for some time, so the taxes you're paying on your income right now might actually be lower.

Other things to think about are big-ticket items that you might want to spend your money on. If you have a tax-free bucket, you might be able to make a large purchase such as a vacation home or an RV to travel around the country. Wouldn't it be nice to be able to make these purchases without having to face extra taxes for the amount of money that you need to withdraw to pay for them? Just look at Janet: She was able to spend extra on a dream trip and help her granddaughter in the same tax year because she had tax diversification.

When to Consider a Roth Conversion

So when is the right time to consider doing a Roth conversion? The trick is to figure out how to use the Roth conversion to take care of taxes when it makes the most sense.

The first thing to look at is your tax bracket. Since you pay taxes on any money converted from a deferred tax account to a Roth IRA, you will want to be in a lower tax bracket when you do this. If you're in either of the lower two tax brackets, a Roth conversion often makes sense. For instance, if you have a lower income tax year, it's definitely a good time to consider doing a Roth conversion. Or perhaps you're between jobs and you're only collecting unemployment.

Here's one way to look at this: If you're in the second tax bracket and you can count another $30,000 as earnings before going into the next tax bracket, then you can convert that $30,000 from a traditional IRA to a Roth IRA. When you move that $30,000 from the traditional IRA, it will count as income and you will pay the taxes on it. But because you will still be in a lower tax bracket, you will pay lower taxes and be in a better situation later because that's $30,000 you will not have to pay taxes on when you withdraw it in retirement. It's unlikely the tax brackets will lower in the future, so by moving the money now, you will have more flexibility and more choices down the road.

Where you pay the taxes from is also an important consideration. Ideally, you'll be able to use money from your after-tax bucket to pay the taxes on the conversion—also known as your cash flow. For example, let's say you decide to convert $10,000 to a Roth IRA and have to pay $3,000 in taxes on that amount. If you pay the $3,000 out of the $10,000, then your conversion will only end up being $7,000—only $7,000 of that $10,000 will be earning income in the Roth IRA tax-free bucket. However, if you can convert the entire $10,000 into the Roth IRA and pull $3,000 from your after-tax assets or your current cash flow to pay the taxes, then you'll have $3,000 more earning income in a tax-free bucket. If that $3,000 comes from a savings account, for example, then you can save taxes down the line in two different ways: In addition to the money growing tax-free in your Roth, it is no longer generating taxable income in the year you did the conversion, so you could see an overall drop in your tax bill.

Another factor to consider about the timing of Roth conversions is this: After you do the conversion, you're not allowed to withdraw the interest on that Roth conversion for five years. If you retired at sixty-five and you're not taking Social Security until age seventy, then consider what your income will be for those five years in between. Once you claim at seventy, then your Social Security will count as income, potentially making your income higher; then, at seventy-three, RMDs will kick in, potentially pushing your income even higher. So, it's best to start Roth conversions as early as possible and during lower-income years.

Yet another factor to consider about the timing of Roth conversions is RMDs (see chapter 9). Currently, RMDs start at age seventy-three; eventually, though, that will move to seventy-five. Roth conversions should be done well before RMDs begin; in fact, Roth conversions should start before you begin collecting Social Security. If your situation allows you to wait until age seventy to claim Social Security, even better, because that gives you even more time to do Roth conversions. Even if you retire at age sixty-five but don't plan to claim Social Security until age seventy, that gives you five additional years to do Roth conversions before your income potentially increases once you claim.

Another question often asked is whether it's better to save in a traditional 401(k) or a Roth 401(k). The answer? It depends! The best time to fix a problem is before it even exists, so, as a general rule, it's a good idea to contribute money to a Roth 401(k) unless you are already in an unusually high tax bracket. The Roth conversion that we just walked through is more of a damage control measure, a way to balance out the three different tax buckets so you don't have a lopsided retirement plan—one with a full bucket of taxable investments and nothing in the tax-free bucket.

However, if you are in a very high bracket, say the 37 percent bracket or the very top bracket, and you also have state taxes in those high brackets, then it may make more sense to stay in a traditional IRA and kick the tax burden down the road to when you might actually be in a lower bracket. Again, with the traditional IRA being deferred, you'll get a tax break today but pay the taxes when you withdraw the money later on. If your income really is going to drop dramatically at some point, then you can do Roth conversions at that time.

Roth Conversions–Not for Everyone

Not everyone needs to do a Roth conversion. If your retirement plan is already balanced between the three different types of tax buckets, then you may not need to do a Roth conversion because you've set yourself up properly in advance. Again, don't do a Roth conversion if it's going to push you into a higher tax bracket today when you could be looking at a lower tax bracket down the line. It doesn't make sense to pay the taxes now at a higher bracket rate when you expect to be in a lower bracket in the future. Perhaps you live in a state with very high taxes but you know you're going to move to a state where there are no taxes on retirement income. For instance, I live in Maryland, but in neighboring Pennsylvania, the taxes are lower—if moving there were in my future, then a Roth conversion might not make sense for me.

Perhaps your 401(k) does not have a Roth component. What then? When it comes to 401(k)s, rule number one is to always contribute at least the amount that your company will match. That's free money; don't let free money fall off the table. But maybe you want to contribute some additional money beyond what you're allowed to put in the 401(k). Well then, create a Roth IRA outside of that.

There are other ways to save money in a Roth IRA, even if you're not fully eligible to do so. For instance, there are Roth IRA contribution limits—the numbers change every year and the break points depend on your age and income. But you can save in a Roth at any time as long as you have earned income, and there is an additional amount you can save if you are over fifty years of age. Currently, it's a $1,000 additional contribution limit, but that's slated to increase. You may not be allowed to save in a Roth if you have a modified adjusted gross income (MAGI) above a certain limit. The numbers that go into calculating your MAGI are too complicated to go into here, but if your MAGI was over $161,000 in 2024, you cannot contribute to a Roth IRA.

Roth Conversions: Strategic Tax Planning for Retirement

Roth conversions offer a powerful strategy for managing retirement taxes, but they're not a one-size-fits-all solution. The keys are timing and understanding your personal financial landscape.

Ideal candidates for Roth conversions are those in lower tax brackets, particularly during years with reduced income—such as between jobs or before claiming Social Security.

Crucial considerations include

- paying conversion taxes from after-tax funds to maximize tax-free growth;

- starting conversions early, ideally before claiming Social Security;

- avoiding conversions that would push you into a higher tax bracket; and

- considering your future state of residence and potential tax implications.

Not everyone needs a Roth conversion. If your retirement portfolio is already balanced across tax buckets, or if you anticipate being in a lower tax bracket in the future, conversion might not make sense. Additionally, those with high current incomes might benefit more from traditional IRA contributions.

Alternative strategies include contributing to a Roth 401(k) if available or establishing a separate Roth IRA. Remember the golden rule: Always contribute enough to get your full employer match in a 401(k).

Keep in mind the current Roth IRA contribution limits. In 2024, individuals with a MAGI over $161,000 could not contribute directly to a Roth IRA. However, those over fifty could make additional catch-up contributions.

The ultimate goal is creating a tax-efficient retirement strategy that provides flexibility and minimizes your long-term tax burden.

Regardless of your tax bracket, you can still do a Roth conversion if it makes sense to do so. But you still need to pay attention to your tax bracket and make an informed decision.

Ask your financial advisor for help with Roth contributions and conversions; advisors understand what is allowed and where you are limited.

ROTH CONVERSION MAKES SENSE	ROTH CONVERSION MAY NOT MAKE SENSE
You expect to be in a higher tax bracket in retirement.	You expect to be in a lower tax bracket in retirement.
You have funds outside the IRA to pay the taxes on the conversion.	You need to use IRA funds to pay the taxes on the conversion.
You want to reduce future RMDs.	You need the money within the next five years and are under fifty-nine and a half years old.
You want to leave a tax-free inheritance to heirs.	You're close to retirement and in your peak earning years.
You have a long time horizon before needing the money.	Your conversion would push you into a much higher tax bracket.
You have years with unusually low income.	You don't have enough cash to pay the taxes on the conversion.
You want more tax diversification in retirement.	You anticipate needing significant tax deductions in retirement.
You've had a year with high deductions or losses.	You expect tax rates to decrease significantly in the future.

Hopefully, you can see the importance of the Roth conversion and when it makes sense to do one. The RRR process we walk through together will bring to light whether it makes sense for you, and then a deeper analysis can be done to implement a plan. In the end, your situation is different from everyone else's, and no one can see into the future, but we can do the best we can right now to try to diversify—not just in your investments but in your tax status as well.

When contributions to a Roth IRA are not allowed for whatever reason, there are other options for investing that offer similar tax characteristics but don't limit your contributions. For instance, an overfunded whole-life insurance policy is something people with high income levels often use. These also offer large tax-free death benefits. If leaving a legacy is one of your number one goals, this might actually be better than a Roth IRA. In the next chapter, we'll take a look at legacy planning—another important part of a retirement plan.

Roth IRA Takeaways ...

- Just like your investments, be sure to diversify your taxes into three buckets:

  □ pretax

  □ tax-free

  □ taxable

- A mix of traditional and Roth IRA accounts can give you flexibility and choices in retirement.

- Look at your tax bracket, and then consider whether you can fill up your bracket in lower earning years by doing a Roth conversion.

- Think differently between ages sixty-five and seventy, and then before RMDs begin.

- Fix the problem before it occurs. Save in Roth now!

CHAPTER 8

Estate Planning

O ur legal system is amazing, intricate, complex, and as a rule, utterly frustrating. For the first twenty years of my career in finance, I was never concerned with what happened to someone's assets after they passed away. But then I found myself working hard to help people invest for income in retirement, put a plan in place to provide for a thirty-year retirement, and ultimately pass assets on as a legacy—only to realize that, without an appropriate estate plan, all of that hard work can go up in smoke. Yet most stockbrokers and big discount broker houses don't talk about estate planning at all; they just seem to ignore it. Don't ignore it. Face it head-on. Otherwise, depending on where you live, you could end up like Diane.

Diane came to my office for an RRR analysis after hearing about it through one of my educational seminars. Her story was shocking. Her husband, Frank, had died at age sixty-four. Frank and Diane had a daughter, Wendy, but it was a second marriage for Frank. He also had a son, Jacob, from a previous marriage. Frank and Diane, for various reasons, did not have the best relationship with Jacob, and there had been no communication between them for over fifteen years.

When Frank died, Diane and Wendy were both justifiably distraught but not too worried about all the paperwork that needed to be done because "everything just passes from Dad to Mom," or so Wendy had professed. For that reason, Frank had never created a will. But they were wrong. Frank was self-employed and, as is common with self-employed people, there were a lot of nonretirement assets in his name—a lot of cash in banks. Seven figures in fact. When Diane and Wendy went to sign the paperwork to retitle the accounts in Diane's name, they were shocked at what happened. In Delaware, where they live, if someone dies with a surviving spouse and with children from someone other than that spouse, the spouse gets half of the intestate assets plus the right to use any intestate real estate for life. Let me translate that. Diane could keep the house and any other real estate she had with Frank. However, half of the cash that was in the bank went to Jacob, Frank's child with his previous wife. Poof! Gone! Legally gone. It doesn't matter what Frank's intentions were; it doesn't matter how many times he and Diane talked about what he wanted to have happen—half of the cash from the estate went right to Jacob.

That's why Diane was in my office. The money that she was anticipating using to generate income throughout retirement was now cut in half. And it happened because there was no will. Spending a few dollars to generate a will would have saved Diane and Wendy over half a million dollars. Diane had to go back to work, only part time, but still, back to work. And money that might have gone to Wendy's future children to help pay for college was also gone.

Estate planning was never on my radar when I was studying finance, but experience has shown me that, as a fiduciary, it is now my job to make sure my clients understand their estate plan. My team of investment professionals at Sound Income Strategies and I work too hard to let what we've built for our clients all disappear because of a poor estate plan. I make sure my clients know that.

Three Phases of Estate Planning

Estate planning occurs in three phases: accumulation, preservation, and distribution. The accumulation phase of your estate plan is pretty obvious: You're saving as much money as you can. The middle phase—preservation—is where I and my team at Sound Income Strategies come in. We look at the fees you're paying over time because when they are excessive, they can reduce the assets you're going to pass on to loved ones. As you know by now, we focus on interest and dividends to help you fund your retirement while protecting the principal. By protecting the principal, we're helping to preserve what you're passing on to beneficiaries. By going through the RRR process, we help clients understand their numbers so that they can preserve the assets that they accumulated in the first phase and that will ultimately be distributed in the final phase. We all know it's important to save money—that's almost instinctual. We all know we need to set up our legal documents accordingly to properly distribute our assets. Sometimes, that's hard to do because it involves thinking about our death and mortality. But don't ignore the preservation phase, otherwise both the accumulation and the distribution phase will be for nothing.

Most people think an estate plan is just for the rich. If you have no money or assets to pass on, then you don't need an estate plan. Otherwise, you do need one, and that estate plan should include a will or trust, an advanced medical directive, and a durable power of attorney for assets. You should include guardianship instructions as well if there are any minors involved.

Probate or Contract Law—Your Choice

Everything you own will be passed on to someone when you die. It's going to be passed on in one of two ways: under probate law or contract law. A good estate plan will allow your entire estate to pass under contract law and avoid probate altogether.

Probate is a legal process whereby an estate is distributed according to your will. With probate, the will is presented to a judge as the last wishes of the deceased; all the state rules surrounding it apply, and it's up to the judge to validate it. The will names an executor, someone who has the legal responsibility to carry out the instructions of the will. Once the will is validated, the executor has the responsibility of executing it. Your executor will essentially pay off any of your debts and then distribute the assets as outlined in the will.

If you don't have a will, dying intestate such as Frank did, then the state has a will for you—as Diane and Wendy discovered. Having a will does not help you avoid probate; in fact, it ensures that you will go through probate.

Probate, while necessary, can be costly and time-consuming. If you have created a will and it goes through probate, the information becomes public. It's a public document that allows anyone to peek into your estate—they can see what's in your will document and then contest it if they want to. They can see how much money you had when you died because it's all public. The reason the will is validated by a judge is so that other people can't contest it; no one can step up and claim it's fake once the judge has validated it.

Contract law is the other way your things will be distributed after your death. Under contract law, your assets will transfer immediately. Contract law is exactly what it sounds like: There's a piece of paper that tells which account goes to which beneficiary. No courts involved, no probate, no publicly displayed assets, no nosy neighbor trying to see how much money you had. Your assets or possessions just move over to the stated beneficiary.

If you have just a few assets, you can add beneficiaries to all accounts, even to your home! Every account can be titled Transfer on Death (TOD) or Pay on Death. Accounts with beneficiaries avoid probate completely, so assets move quickly to the named beneficiary. Retirement accounts fall under contract law, which is why you name a beneficiary to your 401(k), IRA, or Roth IRA accounts. Upon your death, these just pass to the beneficiary or beneficiaries. Whenever we work with a client, we make sure every one of their accounts has a beneficiary added. We work too hard helping people in retirement to let it slip away by ignoring the estate plan.

Given a choice between probate law and contract law, I always recommend contract law.

How Trusts Work

A trust falls under contract law, and while a trust might be appropriate for some people, it isn't required. Going too deep into different kinds of trusts is beyond the scope of this book, but sometimes they make sense because they can be used to pass assets on. Let's just quickly run through how a trust works.

Trusts are used to protect assets, potentially minimize taxes, and avoid probate. Trusts can be revocable, irrevocable, living, testamentary, asset protection, charitable, special needs, spendthrift, and more. Generally, we deal with living trusts, which are created while the grantor is alive, and testamentary trusts, which are created based on the will of a grantor.

A revocable trust creates a contract between the grantor and the beneficiaries. This contract can be changed by you, the grantor, at any point for any reason, hence the term *revocable*. The trust is used for the benefit of those named in the trust.

Once the trust is created, assets are placed in it and the trust owns them. A trustee is named in the trust and is in charge of executing it; the trustee owns nothing in the trust but controls everything in it. While you're alive, you are usually the trustee of the trust. Among the rules stated in the trust are how the trustee is to distribute the assets, including how any money can be spent and what it can be spent on. A trust avoids probate because, when you die, the trust itself doesn't die, hence the term *living trust*.

A quick note: Don't forget to fund your trust. People have come into my office to go through the RRR process and let me know they have a trust. When I go through all the assets with them, we find out that they have a trust, but there's nothing in it. The trust owns nothing. They just assume that when you create a trust, all your assets are in it, but you actually have to retitle your accounts into the name of the trust.

Trusts and wills are completely separate documents. A trust is its own legal document, and a judge never even looks at a trust.

A trust might be appropriate for you, or it might just complicate your life. The order in which assets are distributed is as follows. Assets with a beneficiary assigned are distributed first; if you pass away and have five accounts—savings, IRA, life insurance, etc.—each with a named beneficiary, then those immediately go to those beneficiaries. If there is also a trust with, say, three items in it, then those are distributed according to the terms of the trust. Then let's say there are two accounts with no beneficiaries tied to them; those will be distributed according to the terms of the will. So, if all of your assets are in beneficiary accounts or in a trust, then a will is useless—it does nothing because there is nothing to distribute.

There's more than one way to set up a proper estate plan; what's important is that you have one.

Other Documents

Your estate will also need an advance healthcare directive. According to the Health Insurance Portability and Accountability Act, it is illegal for doctors to give medically identifiable information about you to anyone, including your spouse or children, without your consent. An advance healthcare directive allows doctors to inform the stated family members about your medical conditions. It also allows those family members to potentially give feedback to the doctors regarding your care. This will help ensure that your wishes are followed if you are no longer able to make decisions for yourself. It will also include a list of procedures that you will allow medical professionals to perform in order to save or prolong your life.

A common document that accompanies an advance healthcare directive is a DNR, commonly known as a "do not resuscitate" order. Other instructions can also be included in an advance healthcare directive, such as letting doctors know if you're an organ donor or other things of that nature. An advance healthcare directive is important for many reasons, but one of the most significant is that the people around you might have to make difficult decisions and they're not going to be able to ask you. Don't put them in that situation; create an advance healthcare directive.

Another important legal document is the durable power of attorney for asset management. Should you become incapacitated or unable to handle your own financial matters, the person or entity named in the power of attorney can manage them for you. If you set up a trust, then there is a successor trustee who manages the assets in the trust after you're gone. All of your accounts set up TOD, or those retirement accounts that have beneficiaries, also need someone to potentially manage them if you are unable to. The durable power of attorney gives the people you choose the ability to make decisions and act as if they were you with regard to investments. Often, people with a trust will ensure the successor trustee has power of attorney.

Estate planning helps you navigate your finances. It helps to protect and allow for a smooth transfer of assets at the appropriate time. When I help people create an income plan so their assets will last longer than they do, the estate plan that I push alongside the asset plan is something that my clients may not know is critical at that moment, but it will be when it is implemented later in life.

Estate Planning 101

- Estate planning is the accumulation, preservation, and ultimate distribution of assets.

- The preservation phase is critical—are you spending your interest and dividends or are you spending your principal down to zero?

- Do you have a will or a trust? Are you confident that it's updated for your time in life? Do it now—remember Diane.

- Do you have an advance healthcare directive clearly stating your wishes about your personal healthcare so your loved ones don't have to make hard decisions without knowing your true wishes?

- Do you have a durable power of attorney who can make financial decisions for you in case you are unable to?

- Don't let the state you live in dictate what will happen to your assets. Get your estate plan together using a professional. This is too important to simply write it on a piece of paper and stick it in the top drawer of your desk.

CHAPTER 9

Required Minimum Distributions

RMDs are one of the most underemphasized yet important retirement tools we all need to ensure what every retiree desires—and frankly deserves. RMDs are a stream of income from your investments for the rest of your life.

RMDs are profoundly important because, if you take them the right way, your investments can go a long way toward helping ensure your money will last longer than you. But handling them the wrong way can lead to serious financial mistakes. Even worse, you won't know until it's too late, and then you have the potential of being robbed of the money that you've worked so hard to save. A colleague and friend of mine, Matthew Johnson, often refers to RMDs as "risking my dream," and he's 100 percent right. Don't risk your dream if you don't have to.

What Are RMDs, and Why Do They Exist?

Since 1974, the government has given us an opportunity to invest and save for retirement in accounts that offer different types of tax advantages. Some of that is tax-deferred; some of it can be tax-free.

We know these accounts as IRAs, 401(k)s, 403(b)s, 457s, Roth IRAs, Thrift Savings Plans, and sometimes even other names. These are all known as qualified retirement plans. And while it's a great benefit to have the opportunity to defer taxes while you're working and, theoretically, making more income than you will claim in retirement, at the end of the day, the government wants its taxes. Thus, we now have RMDs.

RMDs refer to the requirement that you start removing your money from qualified retirement plan accounts and pay taxes on those withdrawals. You didn't pay taxes when the money went into the accounts, but you have to pay them when the money comes out. Because of RMDs, you have to take the money out of the accounts whether you want to or not. You have no choice. Wouldn't you rather take those forced withdrawals from interest and dividends instead of depleting your principal? Or would you rather be forced to sell the principal off and distribute it back to yourself? When the rules of investing are turned on their head literally overnight, will your accounts be allocated appropriately to deal with this?

Most financial advisors don't talk about the shift needed to align your assets for RMDs. You need to take these distributions starting at age seventy-three or seventy-five, depending on when you were born. Those born in 1960 or later will be starting RMDs at age seventy-five; everyone else will start RMDs at age seventy-three or have already started them.

The IRS has a table that determines how much you need to take out of your account each year and pay taxes on. This is called the IRS Uniform Lifetime Table, and it can be found in Publication 590-B. This table is the IRS estimate of how long you will live. You take the account balance on December 31 and then divide it by the IRS uniform table estimation of your life, and this is the amount you need to withdraw the next year. The withdrawal rate starts at a little less than 4 percent and then increases each year thereafter. For our discussions in this book, we'll just assume a 4 percent withdrawal rate for your RMD.

UNIFORM LIFETIME TABLE

For use by:
- Unmarried Owners,
- Married Owners Whose Spouses Aren't More Than 10 Years Younger, and
- Married Owners Whose Spouses Aren't the Sole Beneficiaries of Their IRAs.

AGE	DISTRIBUTION PERIOD	AGE	DISTRIBUTION PERIOD
72	27.4	97	7.8
73	26.5	98	7.3
74	25.5	99	6.8
75	24.6	100	6.4
76	23.7	101	6.0
77	22.9	102	5.6
78	22.0	103	5.2
79	21.1	104	4.9
80	20.2	105	4.6
81	19.4	106	4.3
82	18.5	107	4.1
83	17.7	108	3.9
84	16.8	109	3.7
85	16.0	110	3.5
86	15.2	111	3.4
87	14.4	112	3.3
88	13.7	113	3.1
89	12.9	114	3.0
90	12.2	115	2.9
91	11.5	116	2.8
92	10.8	117	2.7
93	10.1	118	2.5
94	9.5	119	2.3
95	8.9	120 and over	2.0
96	8.4		

This all seems simple enough. I have to take money out of the accounts, so who cares how it's invested? Many people have come into my office to go through our RRR process and mentioned that their advisor is using the 4 percent cash flow rule. They are told that they should be able to withdraw 4 percent each year from their account without running the risk of depleting their savings. This sounds easy, and there's all kinds of information out there that says the stock market earns more than 4 percent per year, so no big deal; they'll end up with more money than they started with. But remember the example from chapter 1: When taking 4 percent out of your account every single year from 2000 to 2012, when investing in "safe, low-cost ETF index funds tracking the S&P 500," you would have cannibalized nearly half of your retirement savings in just thirteen years. That would have happened because you didn't make the shift from investing as if you were saving money in that account, rather than investing as if you were distributing money from that account. Imagine waking up one morning and realizing that you have to make it through the rest of your life on half the money you had saved because of how it was invested. That would leave you questioning every expense in retirement, such as taking a vacation or going out to eat.

Again, invest for $TR = I + G$. Invest for the predictable, not the unpredictable. Rather than relying on potential growth to fund your RMD distributions, you can make the shift and invest your assets in instruments that pay greater interest and dividends. If you get growth, great! Isn't that wonderful? But again, you don't need the growth to live the retirement of your dreams. Instead, by investing by contract, as I like to call it, you have a reasonable expectation that the investments you own will pay greater than 4 percent in interest and dividends.

Until you reach the age of RMDs, the government doesn't care whether you take money out of your qualified retirement accounts; it will still tax you based on each withdrawal and it doesn't care whether you make them. But RMDs are forced distributions; when you reach your RMD day, then you must begin taking money out and you must pay taxes on it.

That's why it's important to focus on income first and growth second. If you can take your RMDs from the earnings on your income, then you'll never be forced to deplete your principal so you can weather almost any storm.

The Penalty for Getting It Wrong

As I already mentioned, the key with RMDs is to get it right. If you don't take your RMD before the end of the year, there will be a penalty. Currently, that penalty is 25 percent of the distribution. Let's say you had a $10,000 RMD that you missed. You'll still need to take that $10,000 out, and you'll need to pay taxes on it. Let's say the taxes are $3,000 for both federal and state taxes, and the penalty on the missed RMD is 25 percent—another $2,500. Out of your $10,000 distribution, $5,500 goes to the government and $4,500 goes to you. I promise you will only make this mistake once, and then forever after, you'll take your RMD in a timely manner. We help our clients with this every day.

Also make sure that you prepay the taxes when you take your distributions so you don't get stuck with a bill when you file your taxes in April. Your RMD will be taxed based on your marginal tax rate. This is the highest tax bracket that you fall into.

RMDs could potentially impact your Social Security as well. The amount you take will count as income and, depending on your level of income that year and your marital status, your Social Security could be taxed as much as 85 percent, 50 percent, or not at all (see chapter 6).

Remember that you may be fine for the first years of your retirement, but when the RMDs kick in, then you could find yourself over a threshold and in a higher bracket. For instance, if you're married and filing jointly and your annual income is $40,000, then only 50 percent of your Social Security is taxed as income. The other 50 percent is tax-free. But if you then reach RMD age and have to take an additional $10,000 out of your account, that shows up as income and will push you across the Social Security threshold of $44,000, where 85 percent of your Social Security is now taxable as income. This means that not only is your RMD taxed but you have to pay tax on 35 percent of your Social Security, which you weren't previously paying any tax on—and you have to pay it at the highest marginal rate. Not fair; I get it. But that's the tax code. Be aware of how RMDs might affect your income and plan accordingly.

Dollar Cost Averaging

How can you tell if your investments are allocated properly for RMDs? This is one of the most important topics we discuss during our RRR meetings. We can analyze investments to determine if that critical shift was done to focus on income generation first and growth second. In my years as a financial advisor, failure to make this shift on time is the number one reason people fall short of achieving their retirement goals.

As we are saving money for retirement, we are doing what's called dollar cost averaging. We are putting the same amount of money into the account every two weeks right from our paycheck. If we save $1,000 a month and buy a mutual fund worth $10, then we are buying one hundred shares. But what if that mutual fund loses value? What if it drops down to $5 a share? Well, because we're a long-term investor and don't need the money right away, we're going to save the same $1,000. But this time, we're going to buy two hundred shares. We dollar cost average and buy our shares at an average price of $6.67. Most people would look at this and say we bought some at $5 a share and some at $10 a share; therefore, we paid $7.50. But remember, we bought more shares at $5. Just naturally, by saving the same amount every single time, we are lowering our average buy price. It's good to buy low. Dollar cost averaging saving is powerful.

Dollar Cost Averaging

MONTH	$ AMOUNT	PRICE PER SHARE	# OF SHARES
1	$100	= $10	x 10
2	$100	= $5	x 20

Average Price Per Share = $7.50

= $6.67

Now let's turn that on its head. Let's say we need the money to live on or we need the money to take our RMD. Now, when we need the $1,000, if our mutual fund is $10 a share, we sell one hundred shares and get our $1,000. What if that mutual fund has been cut in half and is now $5 a share? Now we have to sell two hundred shares to get that same $1,000. Now we are selling at $6.67. We are selling on the low. Would you ever implement an investment philosophy that requires you to sell on the low? If your answer is no, then I actively encourage you to go find out how your assets are invested today. Are they generating the interest in dividends to meet your RMD or income needs, or is the government forcing you to sell on the low? Don't sell on the low; I beg you. If your assets are generating that 4 percent or greater yield, you will never have to sell shares on the low because those shares will have generated the income needed to meet your distribution needs.

Are RMDs a Market Buster?

One last comment about RMDs from a very macro point of view. Baby boomers, the age group with the largest population, started taking RMDs in 2016. Every day, thousands of baby boomers reach the age of seventy-three and need to start liquidating shares of their investments to take their RMDs. These same baby boomers are living longer, with many projected to live into their nineties and beyond. Remember that, as we age, our life expectancy goes down and the amount of our RMD goes up. If each year more and more baby boomers have to start taking their RMDs, that means that each year more and more baby boomers will be taking increasingly larger withdrawals from the stock market.

The concern is that as baby boomers liquidate their shares and withdraw from the stock market, it will have an adverse effect on the market. This is a strict economic supply-and-demand lesson. If there are more sellers than buyers, it can drive the price of those goods down. The concern with the stock market and RMDs is that RMDs will force baby boomers to liquidate shares and put downward pressure on the stock market.

Wall Street analysts try to shrug this off and tell us that the next generation of savers—millennials—will step in and invest in the stock market and make up for the baby boomers leaving. I don't readily accept that explanation. We are often shaped by our experiences, particularly our earliest experiences. Millennials' early experiences with the stock market included the 2000 dot-com bubble and the Great Recession of 2008. Watching their parents and grandparents suffer through those two major corrective drops left many of them wary of the stock market. Considering what they witnessed, it's hard for me to believe that they will readily embrace conventional ways of investing and start buying shares of mutual funds. This and the fact that millennials are burdened by large amounts of student loan debt mean that they might not be able to save as quickly as stock market analysts predict. So, millennials filling the void of the mass exodus of baby boomers from the stock market is unlikely. RMDs are a real threat that have the potential to put serious downward pressure on an already overvalued stock market.

This is another reason why I strongly suggest anyone nearing retirement reduce their dependence on investments that require growth and move to investments that produce income in order to have consistent and predictable results.

There's no way you can know for sure if you will be OK financially if you're building your retirement plans on something that is volatile and driven by emotions and unforeseen events somewhere in the world. If you invest by contract, which is often the case with fixed-income investments, you can count on receiving steady income payments.

RMD Takeaways

- Are you generating enough interest and dividends to meet your RMD?

- Will RMDs affect your taxes?

- What can you do today to reduce your RMDs in the future? (See chapter 7 on Roth conversions!)

- It doesn't matter if you need the money or not; the government is forcing you to sell. Are your assets aligned for your phase of life?

- TR = I + G. Now is the time to be income-focused first and growth-focused second.

CHAPTER 10

Choosing a Financial Planner

L et's say you go in for a routine physical and the doctor finds something off, perhaps an indication of some sort of tumor. Generally, at this point, the doctor, often an internist, will recommend a specialist because they're not qualified to treat cancer, let alone your specific medical concern. If this happened to you, you would actively do research, read books, get second opinions, check online sources, and watch YouTube channels about your particular medical issue. That's because no one cares about your health more than you do. Your doctor certainly cares about you and will do the right thing by recommending you move on to a specialist, but, ultimately, you care more about your health than your doctor or anyone else.

For some reason, with our financial well-being, we don't seem to follow the same guidelines. We often just think, *Oh, this person's a financial advisor; I'll just use them; they're all the same.* This is very far from the truth.

There are lots of specialties in the financial advising world. Let's look at how the industry defines financial advisors.

A financial advisor is a professional who provides guidance and expertise to individuals, families, or businesses on various aspects of financial planning and management. Their primary responsibilities typically include:

- assessing clients' financial situations,

- developing personalized financial strategies,

- offering investment advice,

- helping with retirement planning,

- providing guidance on tax strategies,

- assisting with estate planning,

- recommending insurance products, and

- managing investment portfolios.

Financial advisors may work independently, for financial services firms, or as part of banks or insurance companies.

The Financial Industry Regulatory Authority (FINRA) provides a definition for financial professionals, including financial advisors. However, it uses the broader term *investment professional* to encompass various roles in the financial services industry.

According to FINRA, an investment professional is licensed or registered to give investment advice, make securities recommendations, or execute securities transactions. This includes financial advisors as well as brokers, investment advisors, and other financial professionals.

FINRA doesn't use the specific term *financial advisor* in its official definitions because it's not a legally defined term. Instead, it focuses on regulatory categories such as

- broker-dealers,

- registered representatives (often called brokers or stockbrokers),

- investment advisors, and

- investment advisor representatives.

It's worth noting that the term *financial advisor* is often used as a general title in the industry, but it doesn't necessarily indicate a specific license or registration. This is why FINRA encourages investors to look beyond titles and check the specific qualifications, registrations, and licenses of any financial professional they're considering working with.

Just like no one cares about your health more than you do, no one cares about your money more than you do either—not your 401(k) company, your accountant, your neighbor, your broker, your discount brokerage company with low fees—only you. You care about your money the most. And just as you would never accept a doctor's diagnosis of a serious illness without getting a second opinion and doing tremendous research, the same should hold true of someone helping you navigate retirement. Let's look at the various kinds of people who can help you in retirement.

You. You can do your own research and choose your own investments. The question is: Are you financially literate enough and willing to become an expert in the field, or are you just being a gambler? Do you know something about investments and economics and then just check off some boxes to pick mutual funds, or are you truly an expert? Are you hoping your investments will go up so that you have the income you need in retirement?

Discount brokers. These are good for investors who know what they're doing. People who use discount brokers often like to invest and want to put in the time and effort to learn. If you're willing to put in the time to learn, then perhaps you don't need an expert in the field. You might be able to learn enough to get by. But there is one big risk to the do-it-yourself investor: What if you make a mistake and mess up? Well, then you may run out of money before you run out of life, all because of the mindset, "This is no big deal; I can do this myself." Perhaps, or perhaps not. Is it worth the risk?

Robo advisors or robo brokerage firms. In the discount broker world, there are also things called robo advisors or robo brokerage firms. These are really a step sideways from the discount brokerage firms; these robo options have prepackaged investment portfolios that make it look as though you are customizing your own portfolio when the reality is that you are just choosing one out of five or ten different portfolios. Most of these are going to be middle-of-the-road kind of investments that ultimately rely on growth to generate return.

Brokers. There's also a group called brokers. Brokers generally work for large firms, which are often called wire houses. These are going to be the really big names out there that we associate with those who have a lot of money. Advisors who work for the wire houses are really just salespeople. The big wire house has an agenda that it is pushing and hires these brokers to go out and sell that agenda. Often, very little is transparent in what you're getting. You think you're getting financial advice when the reality is you're probably just being sold some sort of product, and if the broker doesn't have what you need, they will just try to sell you whatever they have, which may or may not actually be something best suited to you. Kind of like an internist trying to be a generalist and specialist in dealing with your cancer rather than referring you to a specialist. At the end of the day, it's all about a sale.

The best place to get a specialist is through an independent RIA firm. As I mentioned in chapter 3, this is a fee-only organization that often specializes in unique ways of investing, and the RIA that I am a part of is Sound Income Strategies. Our specialty is right there in the name: income. When you work with an independent RIA such as Sound Income Strategies, your money is held at one of the large institutions, but you will have a personal relationship with a fiduciary advisor who is looking out for your best interests. Your money is always your money; it's always in your name with your beneficiaries. But as the advisor of record, we are able to help position your assets in such a way that you can generate the income needed so that your money lasts longer than you.

No matter where you are, you should understand what's important to you, what goals you're trying to achieve, and what's the best way to get there. If you're trying to generate income in retirement and preserve your assets, make sure that the advisor you work with is a specialist in doing this.

Here are some things that might help you understand if you're working with a specialist who is aligned with your thinking:

- Have you ever asked your advisor to be more conservative with your portfolio but they seem to resist honoring your wishes of moving in a more conservative direction with investments?

- Do you hear them say things like "It's not about timing the market with your money; it's about the amount of time your money is in the market"?

- When the market drops and you voice concern about your portfolio's value, have they ever said to you, "Don't worry; the market always bounces back" or "This time it's different; trust me—it's not the same as the last time"?

- Does your advisor sell some sort of packaged product rather than customizing a plan for you?

If any of these sound familiar to you, your "advisor" is a stockbroker, not an income specialist.

A huge benefit of working with an RIA firm is that there's no financial incentive to recommend some prepackaged product. They're recommending what they believe is in your best interest. It's a fee-based investment philosophy rather than a commission-only investment philosophy.

Beware Bond Mutual Funds

Remember how I talked about corporate and government bonds in chapter 4? Well, a completely different animal, but maybe confusing because of its name, is bond mutual funds. Is your advisor recommending these? Many of today's advisors got into the business in the 1980s or 1990s when the stock market was flying high, and, consequently, they became stock market specialists and typically make these their go-to when investing clients' money. If they do anything pertaining to investing for fixed income, it's an afterthought.

A bond mutual fund is stock that you own of a company that flips bonds for capital appreciation. So if you're trying to fund your retirement, do you want the investment that gives a guarantee of interest payments and the return of your principal, or do you want the stock of a third-party company that flips bonds for growth? Bond mutual funds carry risks and tax complications that can be removed simply by investing directly in individual bonds or other fixed-income securities. As I mentioned previously, when investors buy a bond, they're guaranteed a fixed rate of interest for the rest of the life of the bond, and when the bond matures, they're guaranteed to get that par value back, assuming there have been no defaults. Bond mutual funds do not come with these two very important guarantees. The interest they pay fluctuates, and they never mature, so there is no automatic return of your principal—it's up to you to decide when to get out of them.

If you're approaching retirement or you're in retirement and your advisor is recommending mutual funds, particularly bond mutual funds, it is a clear sign that they're just taking the easy way out. It's easy to check off boxes and then have the mutual funds do all the work. But there's a tradeoff for allowing the mutual fund to do all the work—it's you giving up those important guarantees of return of principal when the bond matures and the fixed rate of interest you will receive over the life of the bond, again, assuming there are no defaults. And, as you know by now, with stock mutual funds, which are focused on growth as a way of achieving return, you're risking market volatility. On top of all this, mutual funds have high costs associated with them. The fees with a mutual fund can be very complex, but they always end up eating away at the gains.

A Question of Allegiance

If your advisor is part of a large Wall Street firm, you need to understand more about that advisor and the firm. Make sure their beliefs align with yours. Is the large Wall Street firm recommending what's best for you or is it recommending its own internally backed products? Where is the advisor's allegiance? Is it to their large firm, or is it to you?

Generally speaking, large firms have younger advisors who are new to the industry. They may think, "The research department is so big here; they're always making the best choice," when the reality is that they're making the best choice for the firm they work for. Is your advisor focused on strictly growing their assets under management? Are you trying to diversify into other types of investments, but all they're willing to do is force you to invest in what they're selling under their brokerage house? Large brokerage firms use assets under management as a way of attracting more people to invest in their firms. Leaving your assets under their brokerage umbrella aids them in their marketing to attract new assets, when perhaps the best thing for you would be diversifying out into different kinds of investments that don't produce as much income, such as CDs, government bonds, or even precious metals.

Step back and take a serious look at your financial advisor: Are they hooked on the stock market? If your advisor says the only way to grow your assets is by investing in the stock market, there might be a serious problem. Period.

While you're working and saving, sure, the stock market is probably the best way to grow your assets. But is it safe now that you're close to retirement? Would it surprise you to learn that large pension funds, which have requirements to pay out huge income to those collecting from them, find stocks too risky? So why do financial advisors always recommend their clients own stocks? Is it because they know something that you don't know, or is it because that's all they know? They probably don't have the knowledge to understand the income-investing world of bonds and bond-like investments.

Other Cautions to Heed

There are a number of other red flags to watch out for when choosing an advisor. For instance, as I've been discussing, is your advisor going to sell shares of your investments to generate the cash flow you need in retirement, or are your investments generating true income? The former can indicate a very, very big problem. Liquidating investments to generate income could lead to you cannibalizing your retirement savings and potentially running out of money. The investment philosophy that you use to save money—dollar cost averaging—helps you lower the purchase price of all your investments. As investments fall, you buy more and more shares. This investment philosophy that works so well to save will work exactly the opposite in retirement. If you're forced to sell more and more shares to generate the income you need in retirement, then you're going to have to sell a greater number of shares when the assets fall. Now you're lowering your average sell price. If your advisor does not understand how this can be devastating to your portfolio, then you need a new advisor right away. Perhaps the stock market will go up enough to recover the money you lost by selling on the low, or perhaps it'll go lower and you'll have to go back to work. Does that sound like a smart way of generating income in retirement? Get out of mutual funds if you're within ten years of retirement or in retirement. If you want to own a bond, own a bond—but don't own a bond mutual fund. If you want to own stocks, great; own stocks that pay dividends so you don't have to sell shares of your investment to provide the income that you need in retirement.

Also be wary of an advisor who is constantly trying to get you to buy an annuity or who is telling you that all annuities are terrible and you should never buy one. Either way, this is an advisor with an agenda. Remember: Annuities are just another tool in the investment toolbox. Understand them—their pluses and their minuses—and then make an informed decision about whether they're something you should invest in.

Does your advisor use a cookie-cutter computer model to do the planning of your assets in retirement? This is another big red flag because every single person's situation is completely different. What might be the right time for one person to retire will not work for another. How much money one person needs will be completely different from how much another person needs. Using some sort of computer model doesn't take into account the variables that are unique to you; a one-size-fits-all system does not know everything about you and your situation. A personal touch is needed.

At the end of the day, choosing a financial advisor is personal. You should take the time to interview multiple financial advisors and understand their investment philosophies. Understand how they're going to generate income in retirement for you and their other clients. After understanding what's important to them and what's important to you, you can then move forward with confidence that your money is being best served.

What Should I Ask My Financial Advisor?

- What is the advisor's education, training, and experience? (Where have they worked and for how long?)

- What is the advisor's basic investment philosophy? They should be able to tell you what to invest in and why you're investing in a particular investment.

- How are you going to get the cash flow needed from your portfolio? Are they selling shares of mutual funds, and where are the investments generating true income?

- Is your advisor happy that you're asking all these questions, or do they seem annoyed? A true advisor will love that you are asking all the important questions! If the advisor is hiding behind "confusing answers," there might be a serious problem.

- How long has this advisor been an independent financial advisor? Without time in the industry, there are a lot of things that they haven't seen. You don't want them to learn at your expense.

CONCLUSION

Any time you venture into unknown territory, you are bound to learn something new. Curious and intelligent people embrace this learning process, even when it's not immediately relevant to their current situation. During my educational years, and most of my working years, I never thought I'd write a book, and yet, here it is. While the process of learning to write was both educational and enjoyable, my ultimate goal is to deliver an essential message about income to those in or approaching retirement. This crucial message, often overlooked during the asset accumulation phase, doesn't receive enough attention as retirement nears. It's a message that the extended family and team of advisors I work with—experts in income-focused investing—consistently emphasize: In retirement, it's all about the income.

While growth is nice, income is essential—it's what we live on and need most. Unlike unpredictable growth, income provides reliability and predictability. This fundamental principle is captured in the equation we introduced in chapter 1: $TR = I + G$, which truly is the answer to every retirement challenge. Throughout the book's ten chapters, you'll find crucial information to transform your retirement from a source of worry into one of ease. When you shift your investment philosophy to prioritize income over growth, the other aspects of retirement naturally align themselves. This income-first approach is vital for every retiree—choosing otherwise means gambling with not only your retirement future but also the legacy you hope to leave. That is a risk that I don't want to take, nor would I let my clients take it.

With a solid income foundation in place, you can confidently pursue your retirement dreams knowing those dreams will become a reality. The RRR process, particularly the dreaming phase, is my favorite part of the work. Seeing people's dreams and lifelong efforts come to fruition because they have the income to do what they had hoped is amazingly uplifting.

To achieve this dream-enabling income, working with the right advisor is crucial. While there are many fiduciaries available—some, of course, better than others—you'll want to find an income specialist. The right fiduciary will help you invest with an income-first, growth-second mindset so that all of your retirement dreams can be actualized.

Income specialists aren't doing anything revolutionary—we use the same investment tools you're familiar with, just differently. Do you think stocks should be part of your portfolio? Yes? Great! Let's make sure you have the right stocks, those that have predictable and reliable dividends. Are we using other investments that have reliable income streams such as bonds or preferred stocks, BDCs, or REITs? Using short-term funds for immediate needs? The full spectrum of income-generating investments must be considered. While there's no magic formula, using these tools strategically can help establish an income-focused retirement portfolio that provides lasting security.

Annuities are one of the most complex and misunderstood investment offerings. But they are just another tool in the toolkit. Understand them and become educated about what they can and can't do for you. Once you have this knowledge, work with an income specialist about whether they belong in your retirement portfolio. If the answer is yes, then do the research to understand what is best for you at the time. If the answer is no, then the good news is that you have made an educated decision based on research.

Social Security, a cornerstone of retirement income, offers various claiming strategies based on your situation. As an income specialist, I made it my mission to understand Social Security and be able to speak the language with my clients to the best of my ability. It is a large piece of everyone's income in retirement. Understand it, understand how it will work for you, understand the pluses and minuses of starting early or waiting, and then make an informed decision and do not look back. While Social Security will be there for you, understanding its role in your income model is crucial—whether you start early or wait, make your choice based on careful analysis of the pros and cons.

Taxes are another unavoidable consideration. Understanding the nuances of today's tax code, particularly that money in your tax-deferred accounts has to be taxed at some point, is essential. If you can understand the fact that the money is not truly yours, you can then begin to work on a plan to "pay it back" to the government.

Some situations call for paying taxes now, others for deferring them—an income specialist can help you determine which approach best suits your circumstances. Understand this, and you understand how all the pieces can work together for you. Understand the power of the Roth IRA and how it might work for you both now and in the future.

Estate planning encompasses the accumulation, preservation, and ultimate distribution of your wealth. Basic requirements include a will, a power of attorney, and an advance healthcare directive—and a trust if it's appropriate for your situation. The will not only helps distribute assets but also helps preserve them. Without a will, your state's default will takes effect, which rarely aligns with personal wishes. Preserving your assets while you're alive by being income-focused first and growth-focused second will allow you to execute on the estate plan that you put in place because now you can make a fairly reasonable assumption that those assets are more likely to outlast you.

RMDs serve as a vital tool for securing what every retiree needs: a predictable lifetime income stream from investments for the rest of their life. The rules have changed now that you have to take money out of your accounts. Make sure your assets align with this phase of life so that they have the best ability to continue to pay you the income that you are now required by law to take. How you spend that income is up to you, but at the end of the day, you're getting it! There's a right way and a wrong way to take income while in retirement; do it the right way.

There are lots of financial planners out there. Look beyond the basics. Understand the different kinds, understand their specialties, and then find an income specialist who can help you generate more than enough income, not just for what you need but for what you want. True retirement success isn't about dying wealthy; it's about having abundant income for life. If you have greater income than you would ever want, then I promise you will have a successful retirement.

You've completed this journey through this book! What's next? Find an income specialist. I would recommend one of the great fiduciary advisors working alongside me at Sound Income Strategies. Go through the RRR process. Understand your income needs versus your income wants, your tax situation, how guaranteed your income is, what kind of risk you are taking today, and what kind of risk you think you should be taking. These important highlights and many others will be brought to light during the RRR process. It will ultimately help you get closer to your money, and one of the most important things you will learn is our most famous equation:

$$TR = I + G.$$

May your retirement journey be filled with success and prosperity.

ACKNOWLEDGMENTS

My first debt is to my children, Rose and James III: I hope to be an example to you both of what it means to be a better and kinder person to all. The joy you bring to my life daily inspires me to create a world worthy of your futures.

To my mother: Thank you for guiding me through life's journey and supporting me even when times were difficult. Your unwavering belief in me has been my anchor through both calm and stormy seas.

To my late father, James F. Locke: I thank you for being someone I can look up to. You taught me that work and dedication to a cause help you grow as a person. I love sharing our name together and the legacy it represents.

To my entire family: Thank you for always giving me the encouragement and time to know I am part of something bigger that binds us all together. The strength I draw from our connections has made this book possible.

To the many friends who help me on a daily basis to laugh and love: Your presence in my life brings a richness that cannot be measured. The conversations, encouragement, and moments of joy we've shared have sustained me through this writing journey.

To my late mentor, Jerry Poole: Though our time together was short, it has helped guide me in ways I could never have imagined. Your wisdom continues to influence my approach to both life and business.

To David Scranton, who saw potential in me that I did not see in myself: Your ongoing mentorship and belief in me is not lost. I think of how lucky I am to have been able to work with you in this amazing business. I am forever grateful for your friendship.

To Christina and Fran and all the people at Sound Income Group: Poole Locke Associates has grown as successful as it is through your hard work and dedication.

To Janet: Your unwavering support and partnership have been the foundation upon which this work was built. Your ability to bring laughter and perspective to our journey together has reminded me daily of what truly matters in life. Your encouragement gave me the confidence to share these investment insights with others. This book, like so many of my endeavors, bears the invisible imprint of your influence and steadfast belief in me.

This book exists because of all of you who have shaped my path and supported my vision for helping others secure their financial futures.

ABOUT THE AUTHOR

James F. Locke is president and owner of Poole Locke Associates, a full-service financial company that has been helping people shift investments to focus on retirement income since 2018. James has been in the financial industry since 1998, beginning his career as an options trader on the floor of the Philadelphia Stock Exchange making markets in equity and proprietary indexed products. He has also worked in the institutional investment sector, helping companies of all sizes manage their data for new institutional investment opportunities.

Today, James strives to educate clients on how to invest for income and avoid losses by utilizing more conservative investment options. His goal is to help people achieve investment portfolios aligned with their current phase of life. James shares this message through educational workshops and webinars specifically focused on income generation and asset preservation.

James holds a Series 65 license and is insurance licensed in his home state of Delaware as well as many states throughout the USA. He has helped hundreds of people maximize the income production of their assets with both stock market and non-stock market investments and financial products. James lives in Wilmington, Delaware, with his children, Rose and James III. The Locke family are avid skiers/snowboarders who enjoy traveling around the United States, experiencing the country's natural beauty while enjoying downhill skiing.

www.ingramcontent.com/pod-product-compliance
Lightning Source LLC
Chambersburg PA
CBHW031403180326
41458CB00043B/6586/J